CHRIS BUSH

Chris Bush is an award-winning playwright, lyricist and theatremaker. Past work includes *The Odyssey*, *Pericles* (National Theatre: Olivier), *Jane Eyre* (Stephen Joseph Theatre/New Vic Theatre), *Fantastically Great Women Who Changed the World* (Kenny Wax, UK tour), *Hungry* (Paines Plough), ~~*Kein*~~ *Weltuntergang* / ~~*Not*~~ *The End of the World* (Schaubühne, Berlin), *Nine Lessons and Carols: Stories for a Long Winter* (Almeida Theatre), *Faustus: That Damned Woman* (Headlong/Lyric Hammersmith/Birmingham Rep), *The Last Noël* (Attic Theatre/ UK tour), *The Assassination of Katie Hopkins* (Theatr Clwyd), *The Changing Room* (NT Connections), *Standing at the Sky's Edge* (Sheffield Theatres/National Theatre/West End), an adaptation of Ibsen's *A Doll's House*, *Rock / Paper / Scissors*, *The Band Plays On*, *Steel*, *What We Wished For, A Dream, The Sheffield Mysteries* (Sheffield Theatres), *Scenes from the End of the World* (Yard/Central School), *A Declaration from the People* (National Theatre: Dorfman) and *Larksong* (New Vic, Stoke-on-Trent). Awards include the Hermitage Major Theater Award, an Olivier Award for Best New Musical, a South Bank Sky Arts Award, three UK Theatre Awards, the Perfect Pitch Award, a Brit Writers' Award and the Theatre Royal Haymarket Writers' Award.

Other Titles in this Series

Chris Bush
THE ASSASSINATION OF KATIE HOPKINS
THE CHANGING ROOM
CHRIS BUSH PLAYS: ONE
A DOLL'S HOUSE *after* Ibsen
FAUSTUS: THAT DAMNED WOMAN
HUNGRY
JANE EYRE *after* Brontë
THE LAST NOËL
ROCK / PAPER / SCISSORS
STANDING AT THE SKY'S EDGE
    with Richard Hawley
STEEL

Jez Butterworth
THE FERRYMAN
JERUSALEM
THE HILLS OF CALIFORNIA
JEZ BUTTERWORTH PLAYS: ONE
JEZ BUTTERWORTH PLAYS: TWO
MOJO
THE NIGHT HERON
PARLOUR SONG
THE RIVER
THE WINTERLING

Caryl Churchill
BLUE HEART
CHURCHILL PLAYS: THREE
CHURCHILL PLAYS: FOUR
CHURCHILL PLAYS: FIVE
CHURCHILL: SHORTS
CLOUD NINE
DING DONG THE WICKED
A DREAM PLAY *after* Strindberg
DRUNK ENOUGH TO SAY I LOVE YOU?
ESCAPED ALONE
FAR AWAY
GLASS. KILL. BLUEBEARD'S FRIENDS. IMP.
HERE WE GO
HOTEL
ICECREAM
LIGHT SHINING IN BUCKINGHAMSHIRE
LOVE AND INFORMATION
MAD FOREST
A NUMBER
PIGS AND DOGS
SEVEN JEWISH CHILDREN
THE SKRIKER
THIS IS A CHAIR
THYESTES *after* Seneca
TRAPS
WHAT IF IF ONLY

Laura Eason
AROUND THE WORLD IN 80 DAYS
    after Jules Verne

Helen Edmundson
ANNA KARENINA *after* Tolstoy
THE CLEARING
CORAM BOY *after* Gavin
GONE TO EARTH *after* Webb
THE HERESY OF LOVE
LIFE IS A DREAM *after* Calderón
QUEEN ANNE
MARY SHELLEY
THE MILL ON THE FLOSS *after* Eliot
ORESTES *after* Euripides
SMALL ISLAND *after* Andrea Levy
SWALLOWS AND AMAZONS *after* Ransome
THÉRÈSE RAQUIN *after* Zola

Mike Kenny
THE RAILWAY CHILDREN *after* E. Nesbit
THE WIND IN THE WILLOWS
    after Kenneth Grahame

Lucy Kirkwood
BEAUTY AND THE BEAST
    with Katie Mitchell
BLOODY WIMMIN
THE CHILDREN
CHIMERICA
HEDDA *after* Ibsen
IT FELT EMPTY WHEN THE HEART
    WENT AT FIRST BUT IT IS
    ALRIGHT NOW
LUCY KIRKWOOD PLAYS: ONE
MOSQUITOES
NSFW
TINDERBOX
THE WELKIN

Evan Placey
CONSENSUAL
GIRLS LIKE THAT
    & OTHER PLAYS FOR TEENAGERS
JEKYLL & HYDE
    after Robert Louis Stevenson
PETER PAN *after* J.M. Barrie
PRONOUN

Jack Thorne
2ND MAY 1997
AFTER LIFE
BUNNY
BURYING YOUR BROTHER IN
    THE PAVEMENT
A CHRISTMAS CAROL *after* Dickens
THE END OF HISTORY...
HOPE
JACK THORNE PLAYS: ONE
JACK THORNE PLAYS: TWO
JUNKYARD
LET THE RIGHT ONE IN
    after John Ajvide Lindqvist
THE MOTIVE AND THE CUE
MYDIDAE
THE SOLID LIFE OF SUGAR WATER
STACY & FANNY AND FAGGOT
WHEN WINSTON WENT TO WAR WITH
    THE WIRELESS
WHEN YOU CURE ME
WOYZECK *after* Büchner

debbie tucker green
BORN BAD
DEBBIE TUCKER GREEN PLAYS: ONE
DIRTY BUTTERFLY
EAR FOR EYE
HANG
NUT
A PROFOUNDLY AFFECTIONATE,
    PASSIONATE DEVOTION TO
    SOMEONE (– *NOUN*)
RANDOM
STONING MARY
TRADE & GENERATIONS
TRUTH AND RECONCILIATION

Russ Tunney
THE WOLVES OF WILLOUGHBY CHASE

Ross Willis
WOLFIE
WONDER BOY

Chris Bush

ROBIN HOOD AND THE CHRISTMAS HEIST

NICK HERN BOOKS

London

www.nickhernbooks.co.uk

A Nick Hern Book

Robin Hood and the Christmas Heist first published in Great Britain as a paperback original in 2024 by Nick Hern Books Limited, The Glasshouse, 49a Goldhawk Road, London W12 8QP

Robin Hood and the Christmas Heist copyright © 2024 Chris Bush

Chris Bush has asserted her right to be identified as the author of this work

Cover design: Muse Creative Communications

Designed and typeset by Nick Hern Books, London
Printed in Great Britain by Mimeo Ltd, Huntingdon, Cambridgeshire PE29 6XX

A CIP catalogue record for this book is available from the British Library

ISBN 978 1 83904 415 1

CAUTION All rights whatsoever in this play are strictly reserved. Requests to reproduce the text in whole or in part should be addressed to the publisher.

Amateur Performing Rights Applications for performance, including readings and excerpts, by amateurs in the English language throughout the world should be addressed to the Performing Rights Manager, Nick Hern Books, The Glasshouse, 49a Goldhawk Road, London W12 8QP, *tel* +44 (0)20 8749 4953, *email* rights@nickhernbooks.co.uk, except as follows:

Australia: ORiGiN Theatrical, Level 1, 213 Clarence Street, Sydney NSW 2000, *tel* +61 (2) 8514 5201, *email* enquiries@originmusic.com.au, *web* www.origintheatrical.com.au

New Zealand: Play Bureau, 20 Rua Street, Mangapapa, Gisborne, 4010, *tel* +64 21 258 3998, *email* info@playbureau.com

United States and Canada: Berlin Associates, as below

Professional Performing Rights Applications for performance by professionals in any medium and in any language throughout the world should be addressed to Berlin Associates, 7 Tyers Gate, London SE1 3HX, *fax* +44 (0)20 7632 5296, *email* agents@berlinassociates.com

No performance of any kind may be given unless a licence has been obtained. Applications should be made before rehearsals begin. Publication of this play does not necessarily indicate its availability for performance.

www.nickhernbooks.co.uk/environmental-policy

Robin Hood and the Christmas Heist was commissioned and first performed at Rose Theatre, Kingston upon Thames, on 6 December 2024 (previews from 30 November), with the following cast:

ROBIN HOOD	Matthew Ganley
MARIAN	Emma Manton
SHERIFF OF NOTTINGHAM	Andrew Whitehead
MUCH	Jodie Cuaresma

All other roles played by members of the Rose Young Company

Music, Orchestrations & Musical Direction	Matt Winkworth
Director	Elin Schofield
Set & Costume Designer	Anisha Fields
Lighting Designer	Jai Morjaria
Sound Designer	Annie May Fletcher
Choreographer & Movement Director	Olivia Shouler
Associate Director	Alex Pritchett
Voice & Dialect Coach	Josh Mathieson
Casting Director	Christopher Worrall CDG
Puppetry Director	Matthew Forbes
Additional Orchestrations	Oli Whitworth
Assistant Choreographers	Irena Cuteric
	Poppydene Lingham

Characters

ROBIN
MARIAN
MUCH, *a balladeer*

WILL SCARLETT
LITTLE JOHN

NUTMEG
CLOVE
BERRY
SPROUT
PEAR
PLUM
PARSNIP
PARTRIDGE

THE SHERIFF OF NOTTINGHAM

BRAMBLE
GORSE

PAGE
COOK

EGG
NOG
SAGE
ONION

PRINCE JOHN
PRINCESS ISABELLA
LORD PICKLE
LORD POTAGE
LORD/LADY MUSTARD
LADY CUSTARD
LADY LARDCAKE
LADY LUNCHEON
LADY PUDDING
LADY PIE

Ensemble parts can be played by actors of any gender, pronouns/titles, etc., changed as appropriate.

This text went to press before the end of rehearsals and so may differ slightly from the play as performed.

ACT ONE

Scene One

Sherwood Forest. Winter. A cold place. Frost on the ground, snow on the branches. We're in a clearing of some sort. A small CHILD *enters, gradually followed by various other* CHILDREN/TEENS. *At the younger end we have* NUTMEG, CLOVE, BERRY *and* SPROUT. *Older children/teens* PEAR, PLUM, PARSNIP *and* PARTRIDGE. *They start to set up camp. They also bring with them paper lanterns in the shapes of houses/other bits and pieces, which they'll spread out across the floor to make a sort of model village – all very natural/ homespun, bits of twig and feather, spare buttons, scraps of fabric, somehow beautiful. There is a sense of industriousness to this too – they're making gifts for loved ones, applying finishing touches.*

MUCH, *a balladeer, is also with them. They start to play, and one* CHILD *starts to sing, gradually joined by the others.*

Song: 'In the Bleak'

MUCH/CHILDREN.
  IN THE BLEAK MIDWINTER
  FROSTY WIND MADE MOAN
  EARTH STOOD HARD AS IRON
  WATER LIKE A STONE
  SNOW HAD FALLEN SNOW ON SNOW
  SNOW ON SNOW
  IN THE BLEAK MIDWINTER
  LONG AGO

  The tune changes – something more rousing/defiant.
  MARIAN *and* LITTLE JOHN *now also join the children.*

COMPANY.
KEEP ON TRUDGING THE SNOW DOWN
KEEP ON STANDING STRONG
KEEP SOME FIRE IN YOUR BELLY
AND IF IT HELPS, A SONG
IN THE WINTER LONG AGO

> MARIAN *breaks off from the group. She sings as an aside – a private moment of worry.*

MARIAN.
LONG AGO THE WORLD SEEMED WARMER
LONG AGO THE WORLD SEEMED KIND
LONG AGO I FELT MUCH BRAVER
SOMEWHERE I WAS LEFT BEHIND

NOWADAYS THE BLEAK MIDWINTER
SEEMS TO LAST THE WHOLE YEAR ROUND
STOKE A FIRE, LIGHT A CANDLE
DRAW A BREATH AND STAND YOUR GROUND

The rest of the COMPANY *join in again.*

COMPANY.
AND IF YOU WANT TO DO SOME GOOD
THEY DRIVE YOU OUT INTO THE WOOD
SO HIDE YOUR FACE BENEATH A HOOD
AND STAND YOUR GROUND!

BERRY (*to* MARIAN). I'm hungry.

MARIAN. I know.

CLOVE. I'm cold.

MARIAN. Take my shawl then. That's beautiful, Nutmeg. Parsnip – can you help him?

> LITTLE JOHN *pulls* MARIAN *aside*.

LITTLE JOHN. Marian? We're almost out of oats. What's left is starting to turn.

MARIAN. I know, John – I know.

LITTLE JOHN. Even the acorns are going.

MARIAN. We'll find something. Robin will think of –

LITTLE JOHN. Robin?

MARIAN. We always think of something.

LITTLE JOHN. I don't know how much longer we'll last out here. If the weather stays like this –

They're interrupted by the sound of a horn being blown.

PLUM. It's Robin! He's back!

MARIAN (*to* LITTLE JOHN). You see. We'll get it sorted.

ROBIN *enters dramatically,* WILL SCARLETT *with him. Music swells again.*

CHILDREN.
KEEP ON TRUDGING THE SNOW DOWN
KEEP ON STANDING TALL
KEEP SOME COURAGE INSIDE YOU
AND IF YOU'RE FEELING SMALL
KNOW WE ALL WERE LONG AGO

ROBIN *also sings an aside.*

ROBIN.
LONG AGO THE WORLD SEEMED BRIGHTER
LONG AGO THE WORLD HAD CHEER
NEVER MEANT TO BE A FIGHTER
NEVER MEANT TO END UP HERE

SO WE FACE ANOTHER WINTER
SOMEHOW BLEAKER THAN BEFORE
SOMEHOW NEEDED MORE THAN EVER
SOMEHOW ALWAYS NEEDING MORE

COMPANY.
AND WHEN YOU TRY TO DO SOME GOOD
THEY DRIVE YOU OUT INTO THE WOOD
SO HIDE YOUR FACE BENEATH A HOOD
AND GO TO WAR!

KEEP ON TRUDGING THE SNOW DOWN
KEEP ON STANDING PROUD
KEEP SOME HOPE FOR THE SUMMER
AND RAISE YOUR VOICE OUT LOUD!

KEEP ON TRUDGING THE SNOW DOWN
KEEP ON STANDING STRONG
KEEP SOME FIRE IN YOUR BELLY
AND IF IT HELPS, A SONG
IN THE WINTER LONG AGO

Song ends.

LITTLE JOHN. Robin, can I have a word?

ROBIN. Can't stop – got to get back to the hunt. Who's coming with me?

PARSNIP. I will.

PARTRIDGE. Me too.

LITTLE JOHN. You've not caught anything yet then?

ROBIN. No, but I have faith.

MARIAN. I'll fetch my bow.

ROBIN. No, someone needs to stay with the little ones.

SPROUT. I'm not a baby.

MARIAN. And I'm not a babysitter.

ROBIN. We won't be long. But we need to go now, while there's still some light.

MARIAN (*sighs – biting her tongue*). Fine. I'll… keep the fire going, I suppose.

CLOVE (*to* ROBIN). What will you hunt?

ROBIN. Hare, maybe. A pheasant if we're lucky.

PLUM. A duck?

PEAR. A goose?

PLUM. A wild boar?

PEAR. A trifle?

PLUM. You can't hunt trifle, stupid.

PEAR. Can't you?

PLUM. No, you only get them in summer.

ROBIN. We're going to do our best, I promise you that. Come on.

> ROBIN, PARSNIP *and* PARTRIDGE *go.* MUCH *might underscore the following.*

BERRY (*to* MARIAN). Tell us again about the feast at the castle.

MARIAN. Ah yes, the Feast of Fools.

MUCH. Everyone in the parish gets invited – they'll come from miles around.

SCARLETT. What if we didn't go?

PEAR. Why wouldn't we go?

SCARLETT. What if we went to protest it instead?

MARIAN. Then you wouldn't get any dinner.

SCARLETT. You know why they do it – why they invite us?

BERRY. Because it's Christmas?

SCARLETT. Because it's a bribe. Let the peasants inside the castle one day a year so we don't storm it the other three hundred and sixty-four. (*To* MARIAN.) Am I wrong?

MARIAN. You can stay here, if you'd prefer to.

SCARLETT. Is that it?

MARIAN. It's a free meal. No one should feel guilty about taking food when they're hungry.

> SCARLETT *is unimpressed by this answer but doesn't push it.*

SPROUT. What will they give us?

MUCH. Oh, mutton, beef, turkey, chicken, pheasant, grouse –

PLUM. Swan.

CLOVE. Really?

PLUM. Yeah. A whole swan on a stick each, that's what I heard.

PEAR. Last year there was even leftovers.

NUTMEG. What's leftovers?

PEAR. It's when you have so much food you can't even finish it all at once.

CLOVE. Marian! Pear's making things up again.

MARIAN. You'll be well fed. That's all that matters.

COMPANY.
WHAT CAN I GIVE HIM?
POOR AS I AM
IF I WERE A SHEPHERD
I WOULD BRING A LAMB
IF I WERE A WISE MAN
I WOULD DO MY PART
BUT WHAT I CAN I GIVE HIM
GIVE HIM MY –

They are cut off by the arrival of THE SHERIFF OF NOTTINGHAM, *and four of his guards/goons*, SAGE, ONION, EGG *and* NOG. *None of them are particularly bright.*

SHERIFF. Halt!

Everyone else freezes.

Well, well, well, what do we have here?

SAGE (*sincerely answering*). Children.

SHERIFF. Yes.

ONION. And an old woman.

SHERIFF. Yes, that's –

EGG. And some sticks.

SHERIFF. Yes, yes, thank you. It was rhetorical.

ACT ONE, SCENE ONE   13

EGG. Some rhetorical sticks.

SHERIFF. No, that's –

NOG. Well, well, well, if it isn't a bunch of rhetoricals.

SHERIFF. Quiet! (*To* MARIAN.) Now, madam, would you kindly state your business here?

MARIAN. And what business is that of yours?

SHERIFF. Forgive me. My name is Nicholas Delancy, newly appointed Sheriff of Nottingham – of which these woods – Sher-wood, the Sheriff's Woods, in their old parlance – fall under my jurisdiction. So, I ask again, what brings you here?

LITTLE JOHN. These woods are free land.

SHERIFF. No, they belong to King and Crown, and I am now their trusted warden. Answer.

MARIAN. We mean no trouble, sir. I'm merely keeping these children entertained.

ONION. Smells funny to me.

SCARLETT. That'll just be your breath.

ONION. Oi – that's assault – that's verbal assault – I'll have you for that.

SCARLETT. Just try it.

MARIAN. Everyone stay calm.

SHERIFF. What is all this? What are you making?

NUTMEG. Ooh – I'm doing a birdhouse –

SPROUT, *the smallest child, holds up a small pinecone covered in glitter – clearly very innocuous.*

SPROUT. This one's for my mum. It's –

EGG. A weapon! It's got a weapon!

SPROUT. It's a hedgehog.

NOG. Hands where I can see them!

SAGE. Drop the pinecone and step away. Nice and slowly.

SPROUT. I can make more – do you want it?

SPROUT holds the pinecone out to them. The GUARDS *panic, and immediately four giant swords/halberds are being pointed at this tiny child.*

NOG. They're escalating! The suspect is escalating!

ONION. Hostile actors identified.

EGG. Prepare to engage with extreme prejudice.

LITTLE JOHN. Hey! Pick on someone your own size!

EGG. Don't you tell me who to pick on!

SHERIFF (*cutting through loudly*). Enough! Stand down!

Everyone stops again. The SHERIFF *leans over* SPROUT.

And what's your name, little urchin?

SPROUT. I'm Sprout.

SHERIFF. Nobody likes sprouts.

SPROUT. My daddy says if people don't like me, maybe they just haven't experienced me in the right environment.

SHERIFF. Is that so? And where is he? Where are all your parents? (*To* MARIAN.) They can't all be yours, can they?

MARIAN. You haven't been in town long, have you, Sheriff?

SHERIFF. Not as it happens.

MARIAN. Then let me fill you in. Adults of Sherwood tend to be in one of three places. Overseas, fighting someone else's crusade; in a field, growing someone else's crops; or in your castle, making someone else's bed. Meanwhile their children get sent out into the forest – left to fend for themselves.

SHERIFF. So what, you're some sort of woodland nanny, are you?

MARIAN. Just someone who helps out where she can.

ACT ONE, SCENE ONE 15

SHERIFF. How very civic-minded. Nonetheless, this is still the King's Forest.

SCARLETT. That's funny – I've never seen him here.

SHERIFF. My, what a tongue you have. It would be a great pity if someone had to cut it out.

MARIAN. Sheriff –

SHERIFF. Hush now, that's enough. I have more important business at hand. (*Flourishing a paper.*) I have an arrest warrant here for the outlaw known as Robin of the Hood, and an arrow of my own with his name etched upon it.

MUCH. It's bad luck to hunt robins, Sheriff.

SHERIFF. I'm not the superstitious sort. (*Beat.*) I'm told he's often spotted in these woods. There's a handsome reward for his capture.

MUCH. We'll let you know.

SHERIFF. Be sure that you do. Remember the law is here to serve you – protect *you*, and these... precious ragamuffins from violent criminals such as he. And of course if anyone were to be found aiding and abetting him, assisting him in any way... it would not end well for them. (*Beat.*) So, does anyone have anything to tell me?

CLOVE *raises a hand*.

PEAR (*hissed at* CLOVE). What're you doing?

SHERIFF (*to* CLOVE). Yes, little one?

CLOVE. Will we really get a whole swan each, at the Feast of Fools?

SHERIFF. The Feast of Fools?

CLOVE. I don't mind sharing, but I'd like to keep the beak.

SHERIFF. Ah yes, I'm familiar with your little tradition, but there'll be no feast this year.

PLUM. What?

SHERIFF. Yes, terribly sad. Cutbacks all round. Responsible leadership requires tough decisions.

MUCH. But we were promised –

SHERIFF. Promised what? Something for nothing? Steal the bread straight out of the King's mouth? No! The gravy train stops here.

NUTMEG. Ooh, will there be gravy?

SHERIFF. Not a sausage.

SPROUT. But I love sausages!

SHERIFF. Silence! Oh, but here's some Christmas cheer – something far better – Prince John himself is coming to town. Yes, thanks to the efforts of yours truly, Sherwood has been chosen as the site of this year's St Stephen's Day Hunt. The finest ranks of English nobility are soon to descend upon us – so alas the banqueting hall is fully booked.

SCARLETT. What?

SHERIFF (*loudly and clearly*). No room at the inn. I'm sure you understand.

MARIAN. You can't do that.

SHERIFF (*shouting*). Don't you tell me what I can't do, peasant! I'm from London!

LITTLE JOHN. But –

SHERIFF. Prince John, *here*, in your fetid little backwater. You should be honoured. You should be kissing my boots! (*To the* GUARDS.) Doesn't it make you proud, boys?

EGG. Will we still get to eat?

SHERIFF. Yes, yes.

NOG. Then we're very proud, sir.

SHERIFF. Excellent. Of course hosting such a prestigious event does put some additional pressure on the public purse. Extra funds must be raised. Every little helps. So…

MUCH. We don't have anything.

SHERIFF. If I had a farthing for every time I'd heard that today! (*To the* GUARDS.) Turn the small ones upside down, then work your way up.

The GUARDS *advance on the group.*

SAGE. Right you are. Hands up – no biting.

LITTLE JOHN. Get off them!

MARIAN (*to the* CHILDREN). Just keep still. (*To the* SHERIFF.) You won't find anything.

EGG. Nothing on this one.

NOG. Or over here.

ONION (*gesturing to the homemade/forest presents*). What about all these?

NOG (*scoffs*). That?

EGG. Just junk. Look at it.

BERRY. It's not junk, it's treasure! It's a house for my daddy. It's where we're all going to live when he gets back from fighting.

SHERIFF (*kneeling down, feigning kindness*). I see. And you made this all yourself?

BERRY. Yes.

SHERIFF. How very clever. How industrious. Well, you're right – it's worth nothing to us. You can hardly pay your taxes in twigs and mud, can you? (*To* NOG.) Any luck?

NOG. Not a penny on them.

MUCH. I told you so.

SHERIFF. No hard feelings. I wouldn't be doing my job if I didn't check. (*Beat.*) Just one final thing – the twigs and the mud – you got them here in the forest, correct?

CLOVE. We foraged.

SHERIFF. Oh how fun! But these *are* the King's Forests, as we've established, which makes this the King's mud, the King's twigs, and you guilty of stealing from the Crown.

MARIAN. Sheriff –

SHERIFF. Which is a capital offence.

SCARLETT. You can't be serious?

SHERIFF. Now, who knows where I'll find the Robin? (*Beat.*) I'll make it worth your while. (*Unpleasantly close to* BERRY.) We could see about getting you that nice house – a real one.

BERRY. You're a bad man and your breath smells.

SHERIFF. Or I could make a nice warm home for you six feet underground.

MARIAN (*stepping very close, revealing a short sword/dagger under her cloak*). Time for you to be going, Sheriff. It gets dangerous in these parts after dark.

SHERIFF. Suit yourselves. (*To the* GUARDS.) Destroy all this. It belongs to the King. Make them an example. Then back to Nottingham – I know they're still holding out on me.

The GUARDS *advance and start smashing up the toys/decorations/models. As they do, a shift in perspective gives the impression that they're also ransacking/working their way through the towns around Sherwood, collecting more taxes for the Sheriff.*

CHILDREN.
IN THE BLEAK, EACH DAY GROWS BLEAKER
AS EACH ONE OF US GROWS WEAKER
SAVE YOUR STRENGTH, WE MIGHT STILL KEEP A
LITTLE HOPE ALIVE

GOD REST YE, TOWN OF NOTTINGHAM
HOW STILL WE SEE THEE LIE
BUT NONE SHALL SLEEP, NO NOT ONE PEEP
THE SHERIFF'S MEN CHARGE BY
AND ANY SIGN OF MERRINESS

IS FOUND IN SHORT SUPPLY
THERE'LL BE NO MORE COMFORT OR JOY
  (COMFORT OR JOY)
NO THEY'LL PUT AN END TO COMFORT AND JOY

Song ends.

Scene Two

The site of destruction at the Great Oak. MARIAN *is trying to comfort the younger children.* ROBIN, PARSNIP *and* PARTRIDGE *have just arrived back after their hunt. They take in the ruin.*

ROBIN. What happened here?

MUCH. The Sheriff came through.

ROBIN. What?

MARIAN. There's a new Sheriff. The worst one yet.

MUCH. I know the old one never helped us, but at least he left us alone. This one…

ROBIN. Why? Why would anyone – ?

MARIAN. He was looking for Robin of the Hood.

ROBIN. Oh.

SCARLETT. We could still catch them – now you're back, ride out and –

MARIAN. No.

LITTLE JOHN. What did you find?

PARTRIDGE. Nothing. Just a dead pigeon.

PLUM. That's something.

PARSNIP. Nah, it was half-rotten already. Most of it was green.

PARTRIDGE (*cheerful*). Oh, but we saw Rudolph.

NUTMEG. What?

PARTRIDGE. You know – Rudolph – the Great Stag of Sherwood. Up by Hangman's Hill. Always good luck, spotting him – it means things are going to change.

PARSNIP. He was looking a bit bony too though.

PARTRIDGE. Doesn't matter – it's only a few days until the feast.

SCARLETT. There isn't a feast any more.

PARTRIDGE. What?

PLUM. The new Sheriff cancelled it.

PARSNIP. No – he can't do that!

ROBIN. Cancelled?

MARIAN. That's right. And he's got other plans for the castle. He's persuaded Prince John and all his cronies to come hunt here on St Stephen's Day.

ROBIN. The Prince – in Sherwood?

MARIAN. That's right. And all his right royal mates. Probably going to have half the wealth of England here in a few days' time.

ROBIN. Oh. Oh well that's... interesting.

MARIAN. Isn't it?

PLUM. Oh, Robin's got that look.

PEAR (*to* ROBIN). What's the plan, boss?

ROBIN. No plan – not tonight, anyway. Let's just get all this cleaned up.

MUCH *starts to play.* SCARLETT *draws* MARIAN *aside.*

SCARLETT. So Robin's going to make a plan, is he?

MARIAN. I'm sure he will.

SCARLETT. The plan you just put in his head? (*Beat.*) Why do you always do that? Why do you let everyone think he's the only one who can save the day?

MARIAN. He's saved us often enough.

SCARLETT. No more often than you have.

MARIAN. We're a team. Everyone's equal beneath the hood.

SCARLETT. We should be taking the fight to them. We should be laying siege to the castle, not hiding out in the woods scrounging for scraps. I *know* you agree with me!

MARIAN. We'll make a plan.

SCARLETT. If the Prince comes hunting here, I'll hunt him. I mean it.

SCARLETT goes. Meanwhile, ROBIN *with* LITTLE JOHN.

LITTLE JOHN. Another sergeant-at-arms came through town last week.

ROBIN. Oh?

LITTLE JOHN. Looking to sign up more men for King Richard's crusades.

ROBIN. And what are they offering?

LITTLE JOHN. Beer and beef. It's more than what we've got here.

ROBIN. We just need to hold out until the spring.

LITTLE JOHN. That's months away.

ROBIN. Solstice night tonight – the longest night – so everything starts to get brighter from now on.

LITTLE JOHN. Robin –

ROBIN. Seeing Rudolph – that was a good sign. Get to bed – we'll think of something.

Everyone else drifts off stage/settles in for the night. ROBIN *and* MARIAN *find a moment.*

So there's a new Sheriff looking for me? What's the reward at now?

MARIAN. Oh, a small fortune, he said.

ROBIN. Maybe you should take it. (*Beat*.) Maybe you should. Make enough to see you all through the winter.

MARIAN. Don't be stupid.

ROBIN. It's not the worst idea.

MARIAN. It's a terrible idea. He'd never pay up.

ROBIN *chuckles*. MARIAN *smiles too*.

So –

ROBIN. Let me guess: the cupboards are empty, the children are scared, and Scarlett wants to wage war on the monarchy – is that the gist of it?

MARIAN. In a nutshell, yes.

ROBIN. You want to go after the Prince?

MARIAN. It's not the kind of opportunity that comes knocking every day.

ROBIN. Could be risky.

MARIAN. We've risked more before.

ROBIN. Have we? Because we'd be risking them too. When we were young –

MARIAN. Don't remind me.

ROBIN. We wouldn't have thought twice. We'd have set off with a quiver full of arrows and a quart of cider and made up a plan on the way. But now –

MARIAN. Now we've got them to think of too – I know. And I don't know how we're going to see them all through the winter – not without something big.

ROBIN. If you think it's the right call –

MARIAN. It has to come from you. You're the one they listen to.

ROBIN. That's not true.

MARIAN. It is. Oh, they might come to me when it's dinnertime, or somebody's stockings need darning, but you're their leader.

ROBIN (*genuinely incredulous*). No I'm not!

MARIAN. Of course you are! It's your name on the arrest warrant! The Sheriff, when he came through here, he would never dream that I could be involved in...

ROBIN. Which was lucky for you, wasn't it?

MARIAN. You know what I mean.

ROBIN. And what do they call me on that warrant? 'Robin of the Hood – outlaw.' I'm on the outside. You're the boss.

MARIAN. You didn't want me to come hunting with you.

ROBIN. Because Parsnip and Partridge are better shots than either of us. Terrifying, those girls. Unstoppable.

MARIAN. But...

ROBIN. Did you really not know you were the leader? Because for an intelligent woman –

MARIAN. No, but all the posters –

ROBIN. Marian, if you want your own poster –

MARIAN. No, and every time I want to get things done, I say: 'Robin thinks this, Robin says that, Robin will come up with something...'

ROBIN. I know. I don't like it when you do that. It gives me heartburn. (*Beat.*) Oh, I got you something.

He produces an apple and hands it to her. She's amazed.

MARIAN. How did you...? Who has apples now?

ROBIN. Plenty in the castle.

MARIAN. You broke into the castle? And all for this?! Robin!

ROBIN. It rolled off a cart! I didn't do anything stupid, I didn't scale the walls. They were unloading crates of them – under armed guard, no less – and this bounced off.

MARIAN. I'll share it with the children in the morning.

ROBIN. What have you eaten today? (*Beat.*) Marian –

MARIAN. What have you?

ROBIN. Okay, I'll split it with you. Things are going to get better, I promise. Spring's going to be here before you know it.

He takes out a small knife and begins to cut up the apple.

I wooed you with apples once, do you remember?

MARIAN. I do.

ROBIN. The sweetest apples in all England – and do you know why they tasted so good?

MARIAN. Because we were young?

ROBIN. Yes, but not only that. There's another reason.

Song: 'The Sweeter Fruit'

ROBIN.
DO YOU KNOW WHY THE FRUIT TASTES SO SWEET?
DO YOU KNOW WHY IT'S SO GOOD TO EAT?
IT'S THE FROST – IT'S THE CHILL
THOUGH IT'S HARSH OUTSIDE STILL
THERE'S A CENTRE OF NECTAR
THAT SOMEHOW GROWS SWEETER AND PURE
THAT'S ONLY BECAUSE OF THE COLD THAT IT HAS
  TO ENDURE

AND IF WE HAD SUMMER THE WHOLE YEAR ROUND
THERE WOULD BE NO APPLES LIKE THIS TO BE
  FOUND
SO PERHAPS, I DON'T KNOW
THERE'S A REASON THE SEASONS MUST COME
AND THEN GO
AND THE SPRING WILL BE WITH US AGAIN

MARIAN. So you still think we should wait it out?

ROBIN. I don't know.

MARIAN. I don't think it's enough.

DO YOU KNOW WHY THE AIR SMELLS SO SWEET?

ROBIN. Go on.

MARIAN.
IT'S BARLEY GONE BAD, IT'S MOULDERING WHEAT
IT'S WHOLE FIELDS LEFT TO ROT
AND NOW ALL THAT WE'VE GOT
IS A LAND GONE TO RUIN
THAT ONCE WAS ABUNDANTLY GREEN
SO TELL ME WHAT SIGNS OF SALVATION
  YOU'RE HOPING YOU'VE SEEN?

NOW WE HAVE WINTER THE WHOLE YEAR ROUND
AND NOTHING WILL GROW IN THIS POOR FROZEN
  GROUND
SO PERHAPS, WHO CAN SAY?
IT MIGHT TAKE MORE THAN WAITING
TO MAKE THE WIND CHANGE
AND THE SPRING TO BE WITH US AGAIN

MARIAN/ROBIN.
AND I –
I NEVER ASKED TO LEAD THEM
I JUST WANT MY FREEDOM
BUT WHILE I'M WAITING FOR A SIGN
I WATCH THEM WITHER ON THE VINE
AND SO IT'S TIME THEY REAP THE SEEDS WE SOW
FROM LITTLE ACORNS MIGHTY OAK TREES GROW!

ROBIN. So are we going to do this?

MARIAN. I'm not sure we have much choice.

MARIAN/ROBIN.
DO YOU KNOW WHY THE FRUIT TASTES SO SWEET?
DO YOU KNOW WHY IT'S SO GOOD TO EAT?

ROBIN.
IT'S THE SOIL, IT'S THE AIR

MARIAN.
IT'S THE TIME, IT'S THE CARE

ROBIN/MARIAN.
IT'S THE PEOPLE WHO GREW IT

WHO KNEW HOW TO NURTURE THE SEED
LEFT NOTHING TO CHANCE TO ENSURE THAT
THEIR HARVEST SUCCEEDS

ROBIN.
AND WE DON'T STOP FIGHTING THE WHOLE YEAR
ROUND
BUT EACH YEAR I FEAR WE'RE STILL LOSING
GROUND

MARIAN.
BUT PERHAPS

ROBIN.
BUT PERHAPS

MARIAN.
IF WE'RE BOLD

ROBIN.
IF WE'RE BOLD

MARIAN.
IF WE MAKE A LAST STAND

ROBIN.
AND DON'T DO AS WE'RE TOLD

ROBIN/MARIAN.
THEN BEFORE WE'RE TOO OLD
MAYBE SPRING WILL BE WITH US AGAIN
YES, BEFORE WE'RE TOO OLD
MAYBE SPRING WILL BE WITH US AGAIN

Song ends.

ROBIN. So then – tell me what you've got so far.

They go.

Scene Three

Nottingham Castle. The SHERIFF *calls for his two aides,* GORSE *and* BRAMBLE.

SHERIFF. Bramble! Gorse!

BRAMBLE. Yes, sir?

GORSE. Here, sir!

SHERIFF. I really need some traction on this. This is royalty. How short are we?

BRAMBLE. Still a few hundred.

SHERIFF. A few *hundred*? What about the churches?

GORSE. They say they've given all they can.

SHERIFF. They always say that! You need to check behind the font, under the pews. (*Off.*) Egg! Nog!

EGG and NOG enter.

EGG. Yes, sir!

NOG. Coming, sir!

SHERIFF. Have you been to the miller? I need another forty loaves by Sunday.

EGG. He says he's still not been paid for last month's grain.

SHERIFF. Tell him Prince John will pay, when he gets here.

NOG. Will he?

SHERIFF. I don't know, just tell him that!

EGG. So lie?

SHERIFF. It's not lying, it's creative problem-solving. Where haven't we looked yet? There must be someone in this godforsaken dump with a bit of cash.

NOG. There's no one in town who earns more than tuppence a day.

SHERIFF. Tuppence! How do you people live?

BRAMBLE. Actually, sire, that's a very pressing issue in –

SHERIFF. I was being rhetorical!

EGG and NOG immediately on high alert.

EGG. Rhetoricals, where?

NOG. Show yourselves!

SHERIFF. Lord give me strength! Prince John has been promised the feast to end all feasts. A dozen wild boar! A sparrow inside a quail inside a partridge in a duck in a chicken in a goose! An ice sculpture of the weeping Virgin Mary!

GORSE. Oh, well the ice sculpture's easy. We just grab someone out of the dungeons, leave them in the moat overnight, they'll be frozen solid by morning.

SHERIFF. Yes, excellent! Practical, economical, I love it.

BRAMBLE. And just how do you get the sparrow inside the quail inside the partridge inside the duck inside the chicken inside the goose?

SHERIFF. I don't know – persuasion?

NOG. We got the mead from the monks. Took a bit of, uh, creative problem-solving ourselves, but…

SHERIFF. What happened?

EGG. Nothing, nothing. Unrelated question – how upset would you be, on a scale of one to ten, if they got you excommunicated?

SHERIFF. Honestly at this point it would hardly register.

NOG. Then we're all good.

BRAMBLE. Now, table runners –

SHERIFF. Oh God!

BRAMBLE. You can have mulberry, garnet, hawthorn, cockscomb, carnation, poinsettia or the red, red blood of Holy Martyrs.

SHERIFF. I need to look at the swatches again.

BRAMBLE. Only we do have the dyers standing by.

SHERIFF. Right, right. What do we think? Martyrs or mulberry? I know *I* want the blood of the Holy Martyrs, but it isn't just about me.

GORSE. Did we rule out holly?

SHERIFF. Holly? *Holly*?! It's not a fifth birthday party, it's the most important social event of the... Honestly, you try and bring a bit of sophistication to the provinces and... Forget it. Mulberry. We're going mulberry – decision made.

BRAMBLE. Great.

EGG. Have we got the man with the funny dog?

SHERIFF. What?

NOG. Oh, haven't you seen him yet? You're in for a treat.

SHERIFF. We shall not be having a man with a funny dog.

EGG. But, sir!

NOG. What about Bjorn the Butcher and his novelty inflated pigs' bladders?

GORSE. Madame Margerie's assortment of amusing root vegetables?

SHERIFF. No! No dogs, no pigs' bladders, no jesters, no jugglers, no bawdy palm-readers. I want classy – I want cosmopolitan – find me a nice harpist.

BRAMBLE. Still looking for a harpist, I'm afraid.

SHERIFF. You know in London you can barely *move* for harpists – one on every street corner.

GORSE. We do have Lady Aria and her Amazing Singing Cat.

SHERIFF. Alright – as a backup – as a last resort.

GORSE. I'll let them know – otherwise she'll get booked elsewhere.

SHERIFF. What else? What else? I need the stables cleaned, the chimneys swept. The tapestries still need updating.

BRAMBLE. The weavers are going as fast as they can.

SHERIFF. You're missing two entire crusades! I will not be made a fool of, okay?

GORSE. And can I just double-check – the meal for the villagers – the Feast of Fools – ?

SHERIFF. We're not doing any of it.

GORSE. Even if we fed them outside, kept them far away from – ?

SHERIFF. Absolutely not. We can't afford it. Do you know how much these lords eat?

BRAMBLE. The larders are well-stocked, sir.

SHERIFF. No can do. I'm bringing *royalty* here, do you understand? If I'm going to rebrand Nottingham as the most fashionable midscale Midlands travel destination of 1192 the last thing I need is any visible locals.

GORSE. Yes, sir, and of course I understand, sir – only I think a lot of the townsfolk might have been relying on the feast, to see them through the winter.

SHERIFF. Then they're idiots. Oh, and another thing – the forest needs clearing. It's full of riff-raff, did you know? Little beggar children – urchins – they all need moving on.

EGG. Where to?

SHERIFF. I don't know! Anywhere. Somewhere no one will see them. Do you think they're the only ones who grew up without parents? The only ones who've faced a cold winter, friendless, alone, trying to make their way in the big city, trying to make a name for themselves in court, thwarted at every turn, laughed at, talked down to, then just when you think you might get a nice retirement gig, Bath maybe, or Canterbury, they send you to the *Midlands*! Can you imagine the indignity?!

BRAMBLE. Is everything alright, sir?

SHERIFF (*recovering*). Yes, yes. It'll all be quite alright. It'll all be worth it, once I've dazzled Prince John. But it all needs to go *perfectly*, do you hear me?

Song: 'The New Broom'

SHERIFF.
 SO THE PRINCE NEEDS CONVINCING
 EVER SINCE MY ARRIVAL
 WE'VE BEEN THRIVING – ALL SMILES
 TO ENSURE MY SURVIVAL

 WE NEED NOTHING TO IMPLY
 EVEN THE SLIGHTEST WHIFF OF TROUBLE
 I'LL REQUIRE EVERY RENEGADE
 IMPRISONED ON THE DOUBLE

 I'LL BE HEEDING NO PLEAS
 THAT THE FEAST IS TRADITION
 SHAN'T SUCCUMB TO SEDITION
 SHAN'T BE SHIFTING MY POSITION

 FOR A CASTLE IS A FORTRESS
 AND WE NEED A SHOW OF MIGHT
 IF THE PAUPERS COME HERE CAP-IN-HAND
 THE GUARDS SHALL SHOOT ON SIGHT

 FOR THIS SMALL TOWN
 NEEDS A BIG MAN
 THESE SMALL MINDS
 NEED A BIG PLAN
 THESE SMALL POTATERS
 NEED AN INNOVATOR
 SO BRING OUT THE BIG 'I AM'

OTHERS.
 (NOTTINGHAM!)

SHERIFF/GUARDS.
 YOU NEED A NEW BROOM – AND ZOOM!

  THEY'LL BE BEGGING FOR THE CHANCE TO
   CHANGE THEIR WAYS
  BRING OUT THE NEW BROOM – KA-BOOM!
  EVERY NOBLEMAN WILL SHOWER ME WITH PRAISE
  WE'LL LEAVE LONDON IN THE DIRT
  DOESN'T MATTER WHO GETS HURT
  GONNA SWEEP UP
  TRY TO KEEP UP
  NO MORE DOOM AND GLOOM
  HERE COMES THE NEW BROOM!

SHERIFF.
  NOW REST ASSURED
  I'LL AFFORD NO DISORDER
  PUT THE POOR TO THE SWORD
  FOR THAT'S HOW THEY'LL REWARD YER

  THEY WARNED ME I MIGHT
  FIND THEIR MANNERS HERE JOLTING
  BUT I NEVER DREAMT THE PEASANTS
  WOULD BE TRULY SO REVOLTING

  STILL THE FACT OF THE MATTER
  IS WE MUST BE EXACTING
  LEARN TO CRACK OUR DETRACTORS
  IF THEY GET TOO DISTRACTING

  IT'S A MATTER OF GOOD GOVERNANCE
  SO HERE'S WHAT I'VE BEEN PLANNING
  GONNA PUT THE KNOT IN NOTTINGHAM
  AND LEAVE THE REBELS HANGING

  FOR THIS SMALL TOWN
  NEEDS A BIG SHIFT
  THESE SMALL FRY
  NEED A BIG FISH
  IT'S SMALL WONDER
  THAT YOU'VE ALL BLUNDERED
  BUT THE ANSWER TO YOUR WISH!

SHERIFF/GUARDS.
  YOU NEED A NEW BROOM – AND ZOOM!

THEY'LL BE BEGGING FOR THE CHANCE TO
   CHANGE THEIR WAYS
BRING OUT THE NEW BROOM – KA-BOOM!
EVERY NOBLEMAN WILL SHOWER ME WITH PRAISE
WE'LL LEAVE LONDON IN THE DIRT
DOESN'T MATTER WHO GETS HURT
GONNA SWEEP UP
TRY TO KEEP UP
NO MORE DOOM AND GLOOM
WE CAN'T START TOO SOON
WATCH THEM CHANGE THEIR TUNE
NOW PEASANTS GIVE ME ROOM
HERE COMES THE NEW
HERE COMES THE NEW
HERE COMES THE NEW BROOOOOM!

Song ends with a big finish. Some commotion offstage. We hear ROBIN (*putting on a very silly posh voice*) *arguing with* SAGE *and* ONION.

ROBIN (*off*). Out of my way!

SAGE (*off*). You can't go in.

ROBIN (*off*). I can and I will!

ONION (*off*). Sir – sir – we've asked you nicely –

ROBIN (*off*). Off with your heads – off with everybody's heads.

SHERIFF. What is that?

As EGG *and* NOG *are about to leave,* ROBIN, *disguised as nobility, enters along with* SAGE *and* ONION. *The* GUARDS *are all a bit flustered. As well as his costume,* ROBIN *has adopted the plummy vowels and unflappable confidence of a member of the ruling classes.*

ROBIN. Aha! Now what have I stumbled upon here? What meeting of curs, rogues and vagabonds? Explain yourselves at once!

SHERIFF. Who are you?

ROBIN. Who am I? Who am *I*? Who are you, sir?

ONION (*to* SHERIFF). We're sorry, sir.

ROBIN. Sorry? I'll show you sorry, my young fellow-me-lad. Now, where might I find the – (*Consulting a letter.*) Silverfish of Rotterdam?

GORSE. The Sheriff of Nottingham?

ROBIN. The Sourface of Nincompoop, that's right.

SHERIFF. How dare you?

ROBIN. You listen here, because I'm not fond of repeating myself – you go and fetch me the Shire Horse of Rotting Ham right now, or there'll be trouble.

EGG (*to* SHERIFF). Shall I just kill him?

ROBIN. Unhand me, scoundrel!

SHERIFF. For the last time, who are you?

ROBIN. Why, I am Sir Percival Peregrine Pontefract, personal attaché and major domo to His Highness Prince John.

SHERIFF (*aghast*). You are?

ROBIN. Dare you doubt it?

SHERIFF. No, sir, of course not, sir.

ROBIN. Then why aren't you kneeling?

SHERIFF (*to the others*). You heard him – all of you, kneel!

ROBIN. No, just you.

SHERIFF. Ah, right. Yes.

The SHERIFF *prostrates himself before* ROBIN.

ROBIN. Now kiss it.

SHERIFF. What?

ROBIN. Kiss my foot.

SHERIFF. Really?

ROBIN. If you value your life.

He does.

Very good. Now to business.

GORSE. You, uh, you said you wanted to see the Sheriff, sir?

ROBIN. Yes. Well no, but it's unavoidable. Ghastly matter. Dastardly. Diabolical. Between you and me, the wretched imbecile is sleepwalking toward disaster, and he's too thick in the head to even know it.

SHERIFF (*horrified*). What?

BRAMBLE (*helpfully*). He said he's too thick in the head to even know it.

ROBIN. Yes, of course simply *everyone* says he's the biggest fool to ever breathe sweet English air. Couldn't hack it in court, that's what they say, that's why he's up here now. Simply couldn't hack it.

SHERIFF. THAT ISN'T TRUE!

ROBIN. I beg your pardon?

SHERIFF. But... but... surely this is all some misunderstanding.

ROBIN. I certainly hope not. The poor soul's to be executed before the week's out.

SHERIFF. No!

ROBIN (*casually*). Oh yes. Or exiled, or clapped in irons. (*Laughs.*) I wouldn't like to be the Shuffleboard of Knickerland right now, let me tell you!

NOG. But what's he done?

ROBIN. Oh, I couldn't break the Prince's confidence.

SHERIFF. Please –

ROBIN. I've said far too much already.

SHERIFF. No, but you must – you must!

ROBIN. Why?

SHERIFF. Because I am the Seahorse of Nazareth! I mean the Sheffield Wednesday. I mean the Sheriff of Nottingham! It is I!!

ROBIN. Oh, but that can't be! You're speaking in full sentences. You haven't got a tail. You smell almost normal.

SHERIFF. Please, sir, I beg you – how I may put this right? I can fix it, I promise. You can't imagine the pressure I've been under. These people, they're so hopeless –

ROBIN. Yes, yes, yes. Tell me, Sheriff, what's your name – your Christian name?

SHERIFF. Nicholas, your benevolence.

ROBIN. Listen, Nitwit, I like you. I'm going to level with you. Prince John has high standards – refined tastes – he's an exacting sort of man.

SHERIFF. Yes, of course, absolutely.

ROBIN. And we're just not sure you're up to the task. Maybe the court doesn't want to visit Sherwood after all. It's not too late to cancel.

SHERIFF. No!

ROBIN. I hear there's good hunting to be had in Richmond –

SHERIFF. Richmond?! Richmond is a cesspit!

ROBIN. Alright, alright, try to keep calm. Here's what we'll do – you're going to talk me through everything, right down to the very last hair – what they'll eat, where they'll sleep, most crucially, how you intend to protect the royal party, and whatever valuables might be about their persons.

SHERIFF. Yes, yes, of course.

ROBIN. And if I'm satisfied – and *only* when I'm satisfied – I'll get everything smoothed over with His Majesty. Now how does that sound?

SHERIFF. Wonderful. Magnificent. I am forever in your service.

ROBIN. Jolly good. Everything must be just so. I mean what do you even have planned by way of entertainment?

GORSE. Lady Aria and her Amazing Singing Cat.

SHERIFF. That's not –

ONION. She's only a little cat, but she's really loud.

ROBIN. Friends, we have much to discuss. Tell me everything.

They go.

Scene Four

Back in Sherwood Forest. ROBIN *taking off his disguise. He's with* MARIAN, MUCH, SCARLETT, CLOVE, NUTMEG, BERRY *and* SPROUT.

SCARLETT. And it worked?

ROBIN. Like a charm.

MUCH. So?

MARIAN. So, it might just be a very merry Christmas after all.

SCARLETT. What did he say?

ROBIN. Right – yes – he said:

The SHERIFF *appears in a different corner of the stage.*

SHERIFF. I'm a nasty man with a big smelly bum and a bum for a brain and when I talk it smells like farts because I talk out of my bum.

The SHERIFF *freezes.*

ROBIN. No, Sprout, that isn't what he said.

SPROUT. Are you sure?

ROBIN. Yes. What he really said was –

The SHERIFF *unfreezes.*

SHERIFF. My bum is so big and so smelly I have to sleep in the stables with the horses but then all the horses died because of my smelly bum.

ROBIN. No, Berry, he didn't say that either.

BERRY. I bet he did though.

ROBIN. No, but the important thing he said was –

The SHERIFF *just makes a prolonged series of farting noises.*

Right! Everyone stop guessing or I'm not going to tell you anything.

CLOVE. Fine!

ROBIN. He actually said –

SHERIFF. Every detail has been accounted for, I assure you.

ROBIN *steps back into the* SHERIFF*'s scene, posh voice and all.*

ROBIN. You're certain?

SHERIFF. I pledge my life on it. Soft beds of the finest eiderdown, enough food to feed an army –

Back in forest.

SPROUT. Did you ask about the swans on a stick?

MUCH. Shush!

With ROBIN/SHERIFF.

SHERIFF. And of course while you feast, a full garrison will be guarding the Prince's gold.

Forest:

NUTMEG. The Prince's gold?

ROBIN/SHERIFF*:*

ROBIN. The Prince's gold?

SHERIFF. Yes, sir – well, rather the gold the lords and ladies are bringing with them as tithes for the Prince.

ROBIN (*bluffing*). Yes, yes, of course – that gold. Carry on.

SHERIFF. Five hundred apiece – is that still what you're expecting?

ROBIN (*almost breaking cover*). Five hundred gold pieces!? (*Recovering.*) Yes, yes. Of course it's very *vulgar* to talk of money out loud, but somewhere in that area. And where do you intend to store this gold while the Prince is here?

SHERIFF. In the keep, sir.

ROBIN. Jolly good. Well, I should make a full inspection – and I'll need guard schedules, schematics, failsafe protocols, all of that. Spare no detail.

SHERIFF. By all means. Follow me.

The SHERIFF *goes.* ROBIN *steps back into the scene in the forest.*

MUCH. Five hundred gold pieces?

MARIAN. Each lord is bringing five hundred with them.

BERRY. Why?

SPROUT. What's a tithe?

SCARLETT. It's money they pay to the Prince so he'll do what they want.

MARIAN. And now we know where they're keeping it.

ROBIN. Oh yes, the Sheriff was extremely thorough.

MUCH. Incredible.

ROBIN. All Marian's idea.

MARIAN. But most brilliantly executed by our Robin.

They share a little kiss.

CLOVE. Er, gross.

SCARLETT. Well then. Merry Christmas to us.

ROBIN. Merry Christmas, Scarlett. Told you something would come up.

MARIAN. Only three days to go – I've got jobs for all of you. We need a map of the whole castle. Pear's mum still works in the kitchens, Partridge has an aunt in the laundry – I've got an idea for that. But the first thing we're going to –

She's interrupted by LITTLE JOHN *running in, breathless.*

LITTLE JOHN. They've got Rudolph!

MUCH. What?

LITTLE JOHN. The Sheriff's men – they came and took him. They're going to hunt him on St Stephen's Day.

NUTMEG. Why?

LITTLE JOHN. Because he's the biggest deer in the whole forest. He's the prize catch.

SPROUT. Not Rudolph!

SCARLETT. But he's a hundred years old – he creaks when he moves – it's not a fair fight.

MUCH. I bet that's why they picked him.

LITTLE JOHN. It is. He looks the part, but they want to give the Prince an easy target.

BERRY (*to the grown-ups*). We're going to save him, aren't we?

ROBIN. We... We're risking a lot at the castle as it is.

CLOVE. But it's Rudolph.

ROBIN. I know. But we have a responsibility towards all of you.

SCARLETT. Marian?

MARIAN. Robin's right. We've got a lot going on already.

BERRY. But I love him.

ROBIN. I'd like to – I'd *love* to, of course I would, but... Well, he's had a good innings, hasn't he? Rudolph's been here longer than any of us. And he'll live on – in our hearts, in our memories – he'll always... You know my dad used to say as long as the last great stag still roamed free, no one here would ever be truly without hope. But perhaps all legends... but the thing is... what I'm really getting at... (*Gives up.*) Yes of course we're going to save him.

MARIAN. Oh thank God.

MUCH. I didn't feel like I could say anything.

ROBIN. So we're all agreed?

ALL. Agreed!

SPROUT. First he broke my hedgehog, now this. He has to pay.

LITTLE JOHN. I'll go get all the others.

LITTLE JOHN runs off.

SCARLETT. I've just got one question though – all these lords and ladies travelling with the Prince – who are they exactly?

Straight into –

Scene Five

A trumpet sounds. The forest clears. Back in the castle, a PAGE *appears. They will introduce a number of finely dressed, larger-than-life aristocracy who enter as they're announced. The* SHERIFF *is also on hand.*

PAGE. All please be upstanding for the arrival of the lords and ladies of the royal hunting party.

SHERIFF. Yes, yes.

PAGE. Lord Pickle.

PICKLE. What, what?

PAGE. Lord Potage.

POTAGE. Pip-pip.

PAGE. Lord[1] Mustard.

MUSTARD. Ahoy-hoy!

PAGE. Lady Custard.

CUSTARD. Tally-ho!

PAGE. Lady Pudding.

PUDDING. How d'you do?

PAGE. Lady Pie.

PIE. Enchanté.

PAGE. Lady Luncheon.

LUNCHEON. Chin-chin.

PAGE. Lady Lardcake.

LARDCAKE. My, my.

PAGE. Countess Isabella.

ISABELLA. Hello.

PAGE. And now welcoming His Most Illustrious Highness, His Royal Majesty and Master of the Hunt, Prince John.

ALL. The Prince! The Prince! Rah, rah, rah!

PRINCE JOHN *and* ISABELLA *don't seem quite as confident as the rest.*

PRINCE JOHN. Marvellous to be here, I'm sure.

SHERIFF (*bowing deeply*). Your marvellousness.

PAGE. The Sheriff of Nottingham, sire.

PRINCE JOHN. Who's that?

PAGE. Our host, Your Majesty.

PRINCE JOHN. Oh yes, yes. (*Over-enunciating.*) Ay up, my duck. Ee by gum.

---

1. Or 'Lady' as cast.

SHERIFF. Ah, very good, Your Highness.

POTAGE (*spotting the* SHERIFF). Nicky, is that you?

SHERIFF. Yes, my lord.

MUSTARD. Old privy-breath himself, is that right?

PUDDING. Oh, is this *that* Nicholas?

MUSTARD. The very same.

SHERIFF. A pleasure to receive you, your excellencies.

PIE. Who is he?

POTAGE. Oh, no one.

CUSTARD. Old Nicholas here fancied himself a big man around court once, didn't you, Nicky?

SHERIFF. That's not –

CUSTARD. Even though he's actually a little orphan nobody.

LUNCHEON. Oh I remember! Bum-licky Nicky – isn't that what they called him?

SHERIFF. I don't think so.

LUNCHEON. Yes, yes, because you were so desperate for everyone to like you.

LARDCAKE. We used to call him 'Old Nick' – do you remember?

PIE. What, because he's the Devil?

LARDLAKE. No, just because he's *really old*.

Boisterous laughter from the others.

PUDDING. Oh, that's priceless.

SHERIFF. Yes, ma'am, the limits of your wit truly have no beginning.

POTAGE. I remember my father used to dress you up in feathers every Easter and then we'd all chase you through the school grounds pelting you with eggs. Good times.

SHERIFF (*through gritted teeth*). Ah yes, good times indeed.

CUSTARD. Couldn't hack it in the big city though, could you, Nicky? Had to hide away out here in the sticks. Isn't that right?

PIE. Hah! Is that so?

CUSTARD. It's what simply everybody says.

PIE. Not everyone's cut out for the cut-and-thrust.

LARDLAKE. I don't know how anyone can stand it here – with only the cows for company.

POTAGE. Well if you've got Nicky's brains, that's probably all you can keep up with.

PICKLE. Now then, now then, let's not be too harsh on the… (*To* SHERIFF.) What are you? The Nightwatchman, or – ?

SHERIFF. The Sheriff, Lord Pickle – I am the Sheriff of Nottingham.

PICKLE. The Sheriff of… wherever we are. No, I'm sure it takes real skill to rise through the ranks to…

He can't carry on any longer – he bursts out laughing.

Sorry! I can't.

CUSTARD. We're only ribbing you, Nicky.

SHERIFF. Yes, ma'am.

MUSTARD. Only joshing.

POTAGE. Only pulling your leg.

LUNCHEON. Only rattling your cage.

PUDDING. Only tickling your salmon.

PICKLE. Only squeezing your weasel.

SHERIFF. Of course.

PIE. Three cheers for the Sheriff.

ALL. The Sheriff! The Sheriff! Rah! Rah! Rah!

LARDCAKE. Now then, whose toenails do you have to pull out to get a drink around here?

SHERIFF. Ah yes, of course. We have a locally sourced honey wine with undertones of geranium and lavender, brewed by Benedictine artisans.

LUNCHEON. *Honey wine?*

SHERIFF. Yes, your ladyship.

LUNCHEON. Well, how very eleventh century.

Laughter from the others.

LARDCAKE. Next thing you know they'll have decorated the banqueting hall in mulberry.

MUSTARD. Here, Sheriff, why don't you go and fetch us some ice from your lake?

SHERIFF. I'm afraid the lake isn't currently frozen over, your grace.

MUSTARD. Then why don't you wade out and stand in it until it is?

More laughter.

PRINCE JOHN. It seems to me the Sheriff has gone to great lengths to welcome us.

The others immediately fall silent.

And so we should not be so grand as to sneer at his hospitality.

LUNCHEON. Yes, Your Highness.

LARDCAKE. Of course, Your Highness.

MUSTARD. Such an excellent point, sire.

PIE. What a good man.

PICKLE. Good old Nicky.

CUSTARD. Wonderful chap.

PUDDING. Salt of the earth – I've always said so.

POTAGE. Three cheers for the –

PRINCE JOHN. Please. Sheriff, I'd like a word with you about the hunt, if I may.

SHERIFF. Of course, Your Majesty. Anything at all.

The SHERIFF *draws slightly aside with* PRINCE JOHN *and* ISABELLA.

PRINCE JOHN. There's a great stag, I hear.

SHERIFF. Oh yes sir, the prize of Sherwood Forest. The jewel of the hunt.

PRINCE JOHN. A, uh, a large creature, is it?

SHERIFF. Oh yes – a most fearsome beast – hooves like anvils, each antler spreads out as wide as a tree branch. It would take quite the man to best him.

PRINCE JOHN (*slightly nervously*). I see.

ISABELLA. But is it safe to pursue it?

SHERIFF. For most mortal men? I wouldn't dare recommend it. But for one of royal blood, and a mighty warrior such as your good husband –

PRINCE JOHN. Yes, well – of course I'd love to, but –

ISABELLA. You don't have anything smaller?

PRINCE JOHN. Just so, uh, you know, the other chaps don't feel left out.

SHERIFF (*pointedly*). Sire, I assure you – the stag is yours for the taking. I have personally seen to it. It presents no threat, but shall make a mighty prize.

PRINCE JOHN. Right, well then… Thank you. Tally-ho, and all that. (*Turning back to the others.*) Uh, three cheers to the stag.

ALL. The stag! The stag! Rah, rah, rah!

PRINCE JOHN. Now perhaps we should all rest, before such an ordeal.

The assembled group drift off. Meanwhile, in the palace stables:

EGG (*offstage*). Easy does it, come on.

EGG *and* NOG *are leading on* RUDOLPH, *a huge deer with massive antlers. Rather than the fearsome beast described, it seems old and a bit doddery.* EGG *is struggling to keep it together.*

Into the warm now – there's a good boy. Mummy's got a nice carrot for you.

NOG. How old is it?

EGG. No one knows for sure.

NOG. Are the antlers tied on with string?

EGG. It's just a precaution.

NOG. And the Prince is really going to hunt *that*?

EGG (*trying to cover the deer's ears*). Don't say the H-word in front of him! Why did they have to pick him? Plenty of young stags they could be going after. But no, the Sheriff claps eyes on Rudolph here and decides that he's the one. Look at him! Wouldn't hurt a fly, old Rudy. The Sheriff wants him wounded too.

NOG. No!

EGG. Yeah, so he'll be easier to catch. I've got a better idea though.

EGG *feeds* RUDOLPH *something from a flask.*

NOG. What's that?

EGG. Honey wine. It'll make him nice and sleepy. (*Back to* RUDOLPH.) Gonna slow you down, and it's a nice way to go out. There you go, drink up, boy. (*Back to* NOG.) I think he's got a bit of a taste for it, if I'm honest.

NOG. Is that why his nose is so red?

EGG. Don't pick on him! (*Trying to fight back tears*.) You'd begrudge him a little drink, knowing what's coming? (*Back to* RUDOLPH.) Right then, let's get you tucked in for the night. I'll sing you a song if you like, read you a story, make sure you're all cosy. You want another carrot? (*Beat*.) Alright, fine, you can have a mince pie, but no brandy butter. Alright, just a spoonful. Come on.

EGG *leads* RUDOLPH *off*. NOG *follows*.

Scene Six

The forest. ROBIN, SCARLETT, MARIAN, MUCH, LITTLE JOHN *and a handful of the younger* CHILDREN.

ROBIN. Everything set?

SCARLETT. You bet.

MARIAN. Everyone knows their positions?

LITTLE JOHN. We're on it.

SCARLETT. Good luck.

ROBIN. Stay safe. And happy hunting.

They disperse. All the various LORDS *and* LADIES *along with* PRINCE JOHN *and* ISABELLA *and the* SHERIFF *enter. Costumes that allude (*however anachronistically*) to the red and white of a Boxing Day Hunt. Obnoxiously high spirits. All are on horseback, however ridiculously this might be achieved.*

SHERIFF. My Liege, I believe it's customary that you do the honours.

PRINCE JOHN. Right. Yes. Excellent. Everybody ready?

LORDS. The hunt! The hunt! Rah, rah, rah!

PRINCE JOHN. Then sound the horn.

A horn is blown.

CUSTARD. Tally-ho!

MUSTARD. Godspeed!

PICKLE. Forward charge!

Song: 'The First Hunt of Christmas'

LORDS/LADIES.
THE FIRST BLOOD OF CHRISTMAS
THE THRILL OF THE CHASE
THE CLATTERING OF MIGHTY HOOVES
THAT MOVE WITH NOBLE GRACE

TWELVE DRUMMERS DRUMMING
KICKING UP A STORM
ELEVEN PIPERS PIPING PIPES
AND HARK THE HUNTER'S HORN
TEN LORDS AND LADIES
LEAP, LEAP, LEAP
A MIGHTY SIGHT
A RIGHTEOUS FIGHT
A MORNING CRISP AND DEEP
HOORAH, HOORAH!
HOORAH, HOORAH!

The LORDS *and* LADIES *all charge off. The* SHERIFF *goes too. The* PRINCE *and* ISABELLA *linger behind.*

ISABELLA. How are you feeling?

PRINCE JOHN. Fine. Absolutely fine. Perfectly fine. Tip-top. Top notch. First rate.

ISABELLA. Are you sure?

PRINCE JOHN (*immediately breaking*). No, of course I'm not!

ISABELLA. We could sit it out.

PRINCE JOHN. No, we can't! No, brother Richard wouldn't like that. I've got to make a show of strength – win them over.

ISABELLA. I could say I had a headache, or…?

PRINCE JOHN. No, there's no way out. Let's just get it over with. (*Half-heartedly.*) Tally-ho.

They ride off.

Meanwhile, SCARLETT *and* LITTLE JOHN *at the stables.* EGG *and* NOG *block their way.*

EGG. Hold it there.

NOG. Stables are out of bounds.

SCARLETT. Alright, take it easy.

LITTLE JOHN. We've got some special instructions from the, uh, the royal horse doctor.

NOG. Oh yeah?

SCARLETT. Yeah, it's about the great stag you're holding.

EGG. Oh! Oh! Does he want to use another one? It's not too late. There are plenty of others. Not Rudolph – he's an innocent –

LITTLE JOHN (*handing over a flask*). They just need you to feed him this.

NOG. He's already finished the mead. He can barely stand as it is.

SCARLETT. No, this is different. Special medicine – it's going to make him feel young again.

EGG. Really?

LITTLE JOHN. But he needs to drink all of it – do you understand?

EGG. Fine! I'll give it to him now. Come on.

EGG *and* NOG *go.*

SCARLETT. Do you know what was really in it?

LITTLE JOHN. Oh, a bit of everything. A lot of horseradish. Ginger. Pepper. Some of those funny mushrooms. It's gonna wake him right up. Just trust the process.

LITTLE JOHN (*sings*).
FIVE HUNDRED GOLD PIECES APIECE
EACH LORD BRINGS FIVE HUNDRED AT LEAST
JUST THINK WHAT A FABULOUS FEAST
THAT WOULD BUY THIS CHRISTMAS!

SCARLETT. Whatever you say!

They go, and more of the MERRY MEN *enter led by* ROBIN.

MERRY/ROBIN.
THE FIRST HUNT OF CHRISTMAS
THE SUN HIGH AND BRIGHT
THE GREAT AND GOOD OF ENGLAND
WORK UP AN APPETITE

EIGHT MAIDS PREPARING
SEVEN ROASTED SWANS
HALF-A-DOZEN GEESE, AT LEAST
FOR THEM TO DINE UPON
TEN LORDS AND LADIES
EAT, EAT, EAT
IT'S NOTHING BUT GREED
FAR MORE THAN THEY NEED
BUT SOON THEY'LL TASTE DEFEAT!

HOORAH, HOORAH!
HOORAH, HOORAH!

ROBIN. This way!

They charge off.

Elsewhere in the forest, the SHERIFF *with* SAGE *and* ONION.

SHERIFF. I know they'll be out here somewhere. Anyone in green – Lincoln green – you shoot on sight.

SAGE. Yes, sir.

SHERIFF. They're not going to ruin this for me!

SHERIFF/GUARDS.
GO FIND THOSE MERRY GENTLEMAN
AND PUT THEM TO THE SWORD
AND THEY WHO FIND THE ROBIN'S NEST
SHALL REAP A RICH REWARD
I'LL BURN THIS FOREST TO THE GROUND
AND YOU CAN BE ASSURED
THERE'LL BE NO TIME FOR COMFORT OR JOY
  (COMFORT OR JOY)
THEY'LL BE NO MORE TIME FOR COMFORT OR JOY!

SHERIFF and GUARDS exit. MARIAN enters with CLOVE, NUTMEG, BERRY and SPROUT. The CHILDREN all wear helmets/hats with antlers strapped to them.

MARIAN. Now be careful. You know what you're doing?

NUTMEG. Outflank them to the east, trick them into following us instead.

SPROUT. Then lead them deep into the forest, and out along the old creek.

MARIAN. And be careful.

BERRY. We'll be too fast – they'll never catch us.

CLOVE. Last one there's a rotten egg!

The CHILDREN run off. MARIAN goes a different way.

The LORDS and LADIES are barrelling down through the forest, trampling everything under foot.

LORDS/LADIES.
THE FIRST BLOOD OF CHRISTMAS
THE KILL MUST BE NEAR
ALL CREATURES OF THE FOREST FLEE
AS SOON AS WE APPEAR!

Suddenly they're surprised by a handful of the MERRY MEN popping up from behind trees/bushes, etc. (ROBIN,

MARIAN, SCARLETT, LITTLE JOHN.) *They fire on them and the* LORDS *scatter. Carnage.*

SCARLETT. Get them!

CUSTARD. A trap! An ambush!

MUSTARD. Run away!

They flee.

ROBIN.
AND PERHAPS

MARIAN.
AND PERHAPS

ROBIN.
IF WE'RE BRAVE

MARIAN.
IF WE'RE BRAVE

ROBIN/MARIAN.
THEN TODAY IS THE DAY THAT THE WEATHER WILL CHANGE!

ROBIN *chases off after them. Full* COMPANY *now present – a mixture of* LORDS, LADIES *and the* MERRY MEN *of the forest, all chasing each other.*

COMPANY.
OH TODAY IS THE DAY THAT THE WEATHER WILL CHANGE
OH TODAY IS THE DAY, OH TODAY IS THE DAY!
TWELVE DRUMMERS DRUMMING!
ELEVEN PIPERS PIPING!
TEN LORDS A-LEAPING!
NINE LADIES CHASING!
EIGHT MAIDS PREPARING!
SEVEN SWANS FOR SERVING!
SIX GEESE IN BACON!

The SHERIFF *emerges. As he sings, the* COMPANY *continue the **countdown**.*

SHERIFF.
   IF **I'VE** BEEN TOO SEVERE
   IT WAS **FOR** A NOBLE CAUSE
   NO **FREE**DOM FOR THOSE FOLK WHO THINK
   THEY'RE **TOO** GOOD FOR THE LAW

   AND WHEN I'VE **WON**
   WHEN I'M DONE
   WHEN I'VE RUN HIM OUT OF TOWN
   WHEN HIS BODY'S IN THE GROUND
   WHEN THE REBEL ROBIN'S FINAL NOTE IS SUNG

   BANG, BANG A DRUM!
   BLOW, BLOW THE HORN!
   HE'LL BE NO MORE!

   The rest of the COMPANY *draw aside/leave.* SHERIFF *is alone. He trains his bow offstage.*

   Come on out. I see you.

   ROBIN *enters, his arms up.*

ROBIN (*in his silly posh voice*). Ah, Sheriff. Fancy seeing you here. What-what?

SHERIFF. Drop the act – I know it's you.

ROBIN. Why, I am Sir Percival Peregrine something-or-other. I forget.

SHERIFF. Don't move! I see you – Robin of the Hood.

ROBIN (*dropping the voice*). Pleasure to meet you, Sheriff.

SHERIFF. No, the pleasure's all mine. You might've outsmarted these country bumpkins for years, but I've got you now. You shan't leave these woods alive.

ROBIN. We'll see.

   He whistles loudly – a beat.

   Just give it a moment.

SHERIFF. You're out of time. If you have any last words, before you meet your –

A scream from the back of the stage. It belongs to PRINCE JOHN, *who runs straight past them and out through the auditorium, leaving through the back of the stalls, screaming blue murder all the while.*

Your Highness?

ROBIN. Here it comes.

Then, following behind from where PRINCE JOHN *enters comes* RUDOLPH THE GREAT STAG. *This is now the fearsome beast that was previously described. His eyes glow red. Steam billows from his nose. He rears up on his hind legs and the* SHERIFF *falls to the ground, cowering, dropping his bow.*

Whoa! Steady on, old boy.

ROBIN *raises a hand to try to calm* RUDOLPH, *who rears up again.*

I know. That potion was a mean trick. I'm sorry. We had to get a little life into you.

RUDOLPH *settles a little.* ROBIN *rummages in a pouch and brings out a bundle of herbs.*

Here – look what I've got – passionflower, peppermint, milk thistle – it'll cool you right down. Would you like that?

RUDOLPH *eats. The* SHERIFF *reaches for his bow or a knife.* ROBIN *kicks it away.*

Easy, Sheriff – the hunt's over – for now, at least.

SHERIFF. I'll find you. We're not done here.

ROBIN. No, not nearly done.

From the shadows, some of the MERRY FOLK *emerge, bows trained at the* SHERIFF.

I'd love to chat some more, Sheriff, but you've got a prince to catch. We'll be seeing you again before the year's out. Off you trot.

The SHERIFF *runs off. The* MERRY *come forward to sing.*

MERRY.
> WHEN YOU TRY TO DO SOME GOOD
> THEY DRIVE YOU OUT INTO THE WOOD
> SO HIDE YOUR FACE BENEATH A HOOD
> AND STAND YOUR GROUND!
>
> KEEP ON TRUDGING THE SNOW DOWN
> KEEP ON RUNNING WILD
> KEEP SOME HOPE FOR THE SUMMER
> AND IF IT TAKES A WHILE
>
> KEEP ON TRUDGING THE SNOW DOWN
> KEEP ON STANDING STRONG
> KEEP SOME FIRE IN YOUR BELLY
> AND IF IT HELPS, A SONG
> IN THE WINTER LONG AGO

Number ends.

End of Act One.

ACT TWO

Scene One

Outside the castle. The younger children, SPROUT, CLOVE, BERRY *and* NUTMEG, *enter through the audience, singing.* MUCH *follows behind, accompanying them.*

Song: 'Wassail'

CHILDREN.
 WASSAIL, WASSAIL WHEN THE AIR IS CHILL
 AND WE SHAN'T STOP TILL WE'VE ATE OUR FILL
 THE NIGHT IS COLD BUT WE'RE SINGING STILL
 WASSAIL! WASSAIL!

 OPEN UP, OPEN UP
 LET US FEAST, LET US SUP
 IN THE DEEP, IN THE DARK
 OPEN YOUR HEART!

 OPEN UP, OPEN UP
 FILL THIS BOWL, FILL THIS CUP,
 IN THE DEPTH OF THE NIGHT
 SEND US HOME WITH LIGHT!

 WASSAIL, WASSAIL AT THE CASTLE DOOR
 OUR HANDS ARE BLUE AND OUR FEET ARE SORE
 OUR MOUTHS ARE DRY BUT WE'LL SING SOME
   MORE
 WASSAIL! WASSAIL!
 WASSAIL! WASSAIL!

This number ends. No response from the castle.

MUCH. No luck. Let's bring out the big guns.

 MUCH *counts them in again.*

CHILDREN.
WE WISH YOU A MERRY CHRISTMAS
WE WISH YOU A MERRY CHRISTMAS
WE WISH YOU A MERRY CHRISTMAS
AND A HAPPY NEW YEAR

SAGE sticks their head out from above.

SAGE. What do you want?

BERRY. We're carolling.

SAGE. What?

BERRY. Carolling!

CLOVE. No, we're *wassailing*.

SAGE. Where's your boat then?

NUTMEG. What?

MUCH. It's a very noble tradition, the wassail.

CLOVE. And now you've got to give us something.

SAGE. For what?

NUTMEG. For the song.

SAGE. No one asked for a song.

CLOVE. That's not the point.

SAGE. Go home, the lot of you!

MUCH gives a nod and they launch into song again.

CHILDREN.
GOOD TIDINGS WE BRING
TO YOU AND YOUR KIN
WE WISH YOU A MERRY CHRISTMAS
AND A HAPPY NEW YEAR

SAGE. Well, uh, same to you. Now go away.

SAGE leaves. The CHILDREN sing louder, encouraging the audience to sing too.

ACT TWO, SCENE ONE

CHILDREN.
NOW BRING US SOME FIGGY PUDDING
NOW BRING US SOME FIGGY PUDDING
NOW BRING US SOME FIGGY PUDDING
AND A CUP OF GOOD CHEER

SAGE returns with ONION.

SAGE. What do you want now?

NUTMEG. Figgy pudding.

ONION. Figgy what?

CHILDREN.
GOOD TIDINGS WE BRING
TO YOU AND YOUR KIN

ONION. Okay, well that's nice, but –

CHILDREN.
GOOD TIDINGS FOR CHRISTMAS
AND A HAPPY NEW YEAR

ONION. Right. Okay, well thank you for that. Thanks very much. Now goodnight.

While this is going on, we now cut to the front of the stage, where MARIAN is explaining the plan to PEAR and PLUM.

PLUM. So they're just going to turn up and start singing?

MARIAN. Sort of.

PEAR. And what's that going to do?

MARIAN. It's all part of the plan. It's just a distraction.

Back to the carolling.

SAGE. What are you still doing here?

MUCH. Just spreading the glad tidings.

BERRY. Now where's our figgy pudding?

SPROUT. And our cup of good cheer?

SAGE (*slowly and clearly*). The. Feast. Has. Been. Cancelled. You. Go. Home. Now.

MUCH. We didn't want to do this, but you've left us no choice.

MUCH *cues the* CHILDREN *again. They sing even louder* –

CHILDREN.
AND WE WON'T GO UNTIL WE'VE GOT SOME
WE WON'T GO UNTIL WE'VE GOT SOME
WE WON'T GO UNTIL WE'VE GOT SOME
SO BRING SOME OUT HERE

ONION. Now listen – you can't just turn up on someone's doorstep in the middle of the night and start demanding elaborate steamed desserts. That's extortion.

EGG *and* NOG *come out*.

EGG. What's all the yelling? Has the cat arrived?

SPROUT. We're not yelling, we're *singing*.

BERRY. Carolling.

SPROUT. Wassailing!

NOG. You can't be – the lake froze over last night.

SAGE. They want some figgy pudding.

EGG. What's that?

SAGE. Search me.

With MARIAN, *etc*.

PLUM. Okay, so then what?

MARIAN. So then all the guards get drawn outside. And meanwhile –

Up on the roof of the castle, ROBIN *with* SCARLETT, LITTLE JOHN, PARSNIP *and* PARTRIDGE.

ROBIN. Now, everyone, try to be quiet.

LITTLE JOHN. I won't fit down there.

PARTRIDGE. You're sure we can't just use a back door?

ROBIN. Too risky. They're on high alert.

PARSNIP slips and yells out.

PARSNIP. Aargh! Sorry – it's icy.

With the younger CHILDREN *and* GUARDS.

NOG. What was that?

CHILDREN (*louder*).
GOOD TIDINGS WE BRING
TO YOU AND –

ONION. Yes, yes, enough of the tidings, thank you!

On the roof...

SCARLETT. So which chimney do we use?

ROBIN. What do you mean?

SCARLETT. Which chimney? There are loads of them.

PARSNIP. What if they've got a fire lit?

PARTRIDGE. Where are we aiming for? Kitchens? Laundry? Armoury?

ROBIN. Just give me a second!

Outside the castle:

SAGE. Come on! (*To* EGG.) You're meant to be up on the battlements.

EGG. I know.

SAGE. No one leaves their post. Go on.

NUTMEG. No, wait –

MARIAN, *etc.*

PEAR. And what if they can't keep them busy?

MARIAN. Then we send in the cavalry.

PLUM. Who's the cavalry?

MARIAN. I thought you'd never ask.

> MARIAN, PEAR *and* PLUM *enter the castle scene*.

MARIAN. Good evening, friends. A merry tune to warm your spirits?

SAGE. Not another one!

ONION. Where are you all coming from?

MUCH. Trust me, you'll like this one – I promise.

Song: 'The Castle Guard'

MUCH.
A WINTER'S NIGHT, THE SNOW FELL DOWN
THE GROUND WAS FROZEN HARD

EGG. Go away!

MUCH.
AND SHIVERING UPON THEIR WATCH
THE HANDSOME CASTLE GUARD

SAGE. Alright. Go on.

MUCH.
THEIR HEART WAS PURE, THEIR AIM WAS TRUE
THEIR ARM WAS QUICK AND STRONG
WHILE WE LIE COSY IN OUR BEDS
THE GUARD STANDS ALL NIGHT LONG

NOG. That is true.

> *The* CHILDREN *join in the song*.

MUCH/CHILDREN.
OH SPARE A THOUGHT FOR CASTLE GUARDS THIS CHRISTMAS
AND GIVE YOUR THANKS FOR EVERYTHING THEY DO
NO BRAVER SOULS THAN CASTLE GUARDS AT CHRISTMAS

WE'LL NEVER KNOW THE TRIALS THAT THEY GO
THROUGH

On the roof.

PARTRIDGE. Hot! Hot! Fire!

Down below.

EGG (*hearing* PARTRIDGE). What was that?

MUCH (*jumping in*).
A HOT, HOT FIRE WITHIN THEIR CHEST
THAT'S STOKED BY RIGHTFUL PRIDE

MARIAN.
THE GOLDEN GLOW OF HONEST WORK
THAT WARMS THEM DEEP INSIDE

On the roof.

PARSNIP. Help, I'm falling!

MUCH (*covering*).
I'M FALLING FOR THE CASTLE GUARD
OH HOW MY HEART'S AFLAME
NOW I HAVE EYES FOR NO ONE ELSE
BUT DO THEY FEEL THE SAME?

MUCH/MARIAN/CHILDREN.
OH WHO MIGHT WED THE CASTLE GUARD THIS
CHRISTMAS?
AND MARRY THEM BENEATH THE MISTLETOE
ALL LONG TO SNAG A CASTLE GUARD FOR
CHRISTMAS
FOR THERE'S NO BETTER MATCH I'LL EVER KNOW

On the roof.

ROBIN. It's this one, I promise – now go quietly!

ROBIN *and his group start making their way off/down
a chimney, making a bit too much noise. Someone falls,
letting out an 'Aaaargh!'* MARIAN, MUCH *and*
CHILDREN *jump on this, stepping up their distraction, now*

dancing with the thoroughly charmed GUARDS *as a way to further keep them occupied. As silly as it can possibly be. First they sing to the tune of 'Jingle Bells':*

MUCH/CHILDREN.
AAAAH THE CASTLE GUARD, THE CASTLE GUARD
THE MERRY CASTLE GUARD
A JOLLY HOLLY YULETIDE SONG
FOR THE HANDSOME CASTLE GUARD!

Then to 'Ding Dong Merrily on High':

GUAAAAAAAAAAAAARDS!
THE HANDSOME CASTLE GUARD

Finally to 'I Saw Three Ships':

I SAW THREE GUARDS COME SAILING IN
ON CHRISTMAS DAY, ON CHRISTMAS DAY
NO ACTUALLY THERE WERE FOUR GUARDS
ON CHRISTMAS DAY IN THE CASTLE!

SPROUT *closes us out, milking it for everything it's worth.*

SPROUT.
OH I WISH I WERE A CASTLE GUARD AT CHRISTMAS
THERE IS TRULY NOTHING I WANT MORE
SO THANK GOD FOR THE CASTLE GUARDS THIS
 CHRISTMAS
AND LET THEM KEEP ALL VILLAINS FROM MY DOOR
FOR CHRISTMAS IS WHAT CASTLE GUARDS ARE FOR
JINGLE BELLS, JINGLE BELLS, JINGLE ALL THE…
 GUARDS

Number ends. The GUARDS *applaud, wiping away tears, truly loving it.*

EGG. Bravo! Bravo!

SAGE. That was beautiful.

ONION. I'm going to go and see about that figgy pudding – you come into the warm.

Into –

Scene Two

Inside the castle. A great fireplace. A lot of commotion, then ROBIN, SCARLETT, LITTLE JOHN, PARSNIP *and* PARTRIDGE *all thud down the chimney one by one, sprawling on the ground. They take a moment to compose themselves.*

ROBIN. Everyone alright?

PARSNIP. Where are we?

LITTLE JOHN. Servants' quarters.

SCARLETT. No chance they'd have a fire lit here.

ROBIN. All the guests should be in the banqueting hall. Now, Partridge – did you sort out those disguises?

PARTRIDGE. Oh right, yeah, my aunt should've hidden us a parcel somewhere.

LITTLE JOHN. Your aunt?

PARTRIDGE *(looking around)*. Yeah, she works in the laundry – she's leaving us out some guard uniforms so later we can...

PARTRIDGE *finds the bag and looks inside.*

Ah.

PARSNIP. What is it?

PARTRIDGE. Nothing.

ROBIN. Is there a problem?

PARTRIDGE. No. It's very thoughtful actually. It's funny. You'll laugh.

SCARLETT. What is it?

PARTRIDGE *pulls out a number of brightly coloured stockings from the sack.*

PARTRIDGE. She knits us socks every year – well, every year she can get the fabric. Oh look – they're *made* from old guard uniforms! You can see the braiding –

PARSNIP. What are we meant to do with these?

PARTRIDGE. Yeah, I think she misunderstood the brief.

SCARLETT. Why would she think you were asking for extra-long novelty socks?

PARTRIDGE. Because it's Christmas!

ROBIN. Right, right, well we can… we'll use them to carry our treasure in, maybe? We'll take them with us. (*To* PARSNIP.) Now, have you got the bait?

PARSNIP. Yep. Honey cakes, just as you ordered. Plum's mum made them.

PARTRIDGE. Ooh, let's try one!

ROBIN. No!

PARTRIDGE. But –

PARSNIP. There's enough valerian root in them to make you sleep until New Year.

LITTLE JOHN. Do you really think professional castle guards are going to eat some random bit of cake they find lying around by a fireplace?

PARSNIP. We've got milk too – and I've done a note.

PARTRIDGE. What does it say?

PARSNIP. 'Dear castle guards, please drink this milk and eat this cake. Merry Christmas.'

SCARLETT. Oh, well that's foolproof then.

ROBIN. It doesn't hurt to try. Now come on, let's check out this banquet.

PARSNIP puts out the milk, cookies and note. ROBIN *leads them off. A few moments later,* EGG *and* NOG *enter from another direction.*

EGG. I'm telling you, I heard something.

NOG. Alright, let's see. (*Spotting the milk.*) What's that?

EGG (*reading the note*). 'Dear castle guards'... Oh! It's for us!

NOG. Is it?

EGG. Yeah – look!

NOG (*reading the note*). Wow.

EGG. And with the singing too – cos I've been doing this job a while, and it's not easy –

NOG. Tell me about it.

EGG. And I've been... Ooh, I'm getting a bit emotional actually. I'm welling up.

NOG. That's alright. You let it out.

EGG. Because you know, everyone's always like 'you're the bad guy' and 'why are you doing this?' and 'stop poking me with that red-hot poker.'

NOG. People are *always* saying that.

EGG. But nobody ever asks how does it feel to be doing the poking, you know? What's the emotional burden of that?

NOG. You're so right.

EGG. But days like today – they really restore your faith, y'know? Really makes you feel appreciated. Best Christmas ever.

NOG. Best Christmas ever. Come on – let's share these round.

They go, already munching cakes as they leave.

Scene Three

The banqueting hall. The various LORDS *and* LADIES *pile in, along with the* SHERIFF, PRINCE JOHN *and* ISABELLA. *The* PRINCE *has a blanket around his shoulders and has clearly been through something. All the* LORDS *and* LADIES *seem a little frazzled.*

PRINCE JOHN. Did you see it?

SHERIFF. Yes, My Liege.

PRINCE JOHN. That was no ordinary deer.

ISABELLA (*hissed to the* SHERIFF). You promised him –

PRINCE JOHN. Twelve feet tall, at least. Sent by the Devil himself.

ISABELLA. You were very brave.

PRINCE JOHN. Yes I was, wasn't I?

PUDDING. What happened out there?

PIE. Who were those people?

SHERIFF. Nobody, your ladyship. Commoners. Agitators. The situation is in hand.

MUSTARD. Didn't seem very in hand, Nicky.

LARDCAKE. All a bit much for you, is it? A bit beyond your capabilities?

CUSTARD. What's the situation here – do you have a line manager?

SHERIFF. Please, your lords, your ladyships, I understand your concerns. And may I just say thank heavens for the Prince, or we would've all been doomed.

ISABELLA. We would?

SHERIFF. Of course His Highness is too humble to say so himself. But I saw everything.

PRINCE JOHN. You did?

SHERIFF. Yes, sire. You see this wasn't just a local domestic threat – oh no. Assassins, sent from overseas no doubt, working with pagan communist necromancers to make an attempt on the Prince's life.

PICKLE. Really?

SHERIFF. Oh, absolutely. You all saw the creature?

PRINCE JOHN. I did! I saw it!

SHERIFF. And was it any ordinary stag?

PRINCE JOHN. No it was not!

SHERIFF. No, My Liege, but a magical beast summoned straight from the bowels of hell, imbued with such ungodly power it would've surely slaughtered us all. But then the Prince, in a display of heroism that will surely echo throughout the ages, drove the foul creature back into the forest, back into the infernal plane, saving not just all your lives, but in all likelihood the very soul of England itself.

LUNCHEON. Gosh.

PRINCE JOHN. Yes. I did that. That's exactly what happened. I just didn't want to make a fuss.

PICKLE. Well then – to the Prince.

The group aren't entirely buying this, but they make the toast anyway.

ALL. The Prince! The Prince! Rah, rah, rah!

PRINCE JOHN. I'm sure any of you would've done the same. (*Pressing his advantage.*) But speaking of what you can do, I believe you have all brought some contributions with you, to ensure the country's smooth running in my brother's absence?

POTAGE. We have, sire.

PRINCE JOHN. Excellent. And of course I'm eager to hear any thoughts or concerns you might have. (*To the* SHERIFF.) I trust the funds are all safely secured?

SHERIFF. Yes, sire – in the keep – utterly impenetrable.

PRINCE JOHN. Excellent. But before we get to that –

On this, a commotion offstage and MUCH *and* MARIAN *(partially disguised) enter with* SPROUT, CLOVE, BERRY *and* NUTMEG. SAGE *and* ONION *follow on behind, seemingly a little out of it.* MUCH *has adopted a bad cockney accent.*

MUCH. Greetings, my lords, my ladies, Your Highness.

SHERIFF. What's all this?

ONION. Now… now hear them out.

SAGE. They're actually very talented. (*Yawns.*) Is anyone else getting sleepy?

PUDDING. Are you the entertainment?

MUCH. That's right, my lady. Come all the way from London, so we have. Cor blimey, guv'nor.

SHERIFF. Really?

PIE. What do you do?

BERRY. We're here to tell you the true story of Christmas.

MUSTARD. Oh no, are they travelling players?

PICKLE. You hired actors?

PIE. Even worse – *child* actors.

MUSTARD. Don't you have a man with a funny dog?

NUTMEG. This is the story of the birth of Our Lord and Saviour Jesus Christ.

LUNCHEON. Bo-ring.

MUCH. Of course if there are any heathens here who *aren't* interested in Our Lord and Saviour Jesus Christ –

LUNCHEON. No, no, you're right – go ahead.

The CHILDREN *start performing a fairly bad nativity play.*

ACT TWO, SCENE THREE 71

NUTMEG. Ahem. Long time ago in Bethlehem, so the Holy Bible say –

POTAGE. Ugh.

LARDCAKE. Shush.

NUTMEG. Mary and Joseph lived in the town of Nazareth, ruled over by the wicked King Herod.

SPROUT. I am King Herod. I like breaking things for no reason and I have a stinky bum.

MUSTARD (*laughing heartily*). Oh, that's very good – that's *satire*.

NUTMEG *nudges* SPROUT.

NUTMEG. Do it properly!

SPROUT. Fine. I am King Herod. I need to know the names of everybody in my kingdom so they can all pay their proper taxes.

PICKLE. Good, good! Very important!

SPROUT. So everyone must now go back to their home towns to be counted.

NUTMEG. Mary and Joseph prepared to travel to Bethlehem, but before they left, they were visited by an angel.

CLOVE (*as angel*). Mary, be not afraid. God has chosen you for a great honour. You are to carry his child. You shall name him Jesus, and he shall be the saviour of the world.

SHERIFF. Yes, yes, I think we know the rest. Bethlehem, follow the star, virgin birth – if we could wrap this up?

BERRY. But we're not finished!

NUTMEG. We haven't even got to the shepherds yet.

CLOVE. Or the wise men.

SPROUT. Or the cattle a-lowing.

BERRY (*waving to* CLOVE). Allo!

CLOVE (*waving back*). Allo!

SPROUT. No – *lowing*. Looooooooow!

The others join in, 'lowing' like cows.

CHILDREN (*louder*). LOOOOOOOOW!

SHERIFF. Stop it!

SAGE. Ooh! Ooh! Do the castle guard song again!

SHERIFF. No thank you! (*Stepping in.*) Right, a round of applause for the small children who can partially remember the story of the birth of Jesus. Now then –

MUCH. How about a merry jig?

CLOVE. We know a song about a donkey.

SHERIFF. Why would anybody want a song about a donkey? No – you know what, forget I asked – thank you so much for your time – don't touch anything on your way out.

MUCH (*to* MARIAN). What do we do?

MARIAN. I don't know – we still need to stall them.

SHERIFF. What was that?

MUCH. Sheriff, why don't you give us a tune?

SHERIFF. Oh, I couldn't possibly.

MARIAN. Go on – show us how it's done.

SHERIFF. Well it's been a while. I'm sure I couldn't…

The SHERIFF *produces a violin and immediately plays a very impressive flourish of music.*

Alright then, it's time to strip the willow, then the Eightsome Reel into St Bernard's Waltz – and a one, and a two… (*Stopping himself.*) Hold on – I recognise you. You're the troublemakers from the forest!

MARIAN. Right – plan B.

MARIAN *produces a horn and blows it loudly.*

ISABELLA. What's going on?

PUDDING. Pagan communist necromancers!

CUSTARD. They're coming for the children too!

A commotion offstage. The voice of a COOK.

COOK *(offstage)*. Fire! Fire!

SHERIFF. Guards!

The COOK crashes in, holding a flaming Christmas pudding. Chaos ensues.

COOK. Someone set the pudding on fire!

PIE. We're under attack!

MARIAN. Run!

SHERIFF. Seize them!

ISABELLA. Protect your Prince!

PICKLE. No, save yourselves!

The LORDS and LADIES start to pile out. A GUARD (helmet obscuring their face) comes to bundle out PRINCE JOHN and ISABELLA.

GUARD 1. Your Majesty – this way! Come with us.

The PRINCE and ISABELLA leave with the GUARD.

MARIAN. So long, Sheriff.

MARIAN *goes a different way – the* SHERIFF *pursues.*

A number that moves us out of the castle and out into the forest. Driving, propulsive, matching the fast rhythm of horse's hooves.

Song: 'Wassail (Reprise)'

COMPANY.
WASSAIL! WASSAIL! ON A WINTER'S NIGHT
THE AIR IS CHILL AND THE STARS ARE BRIGHT
THE ROAD IS LONG SO HOLD ON TIGHT
WASSAIL! WASSAIL!

A carriage is formed in front of us. A hooded DRIVER *holds the reins. The* GUARD *returns with* PRINCE JOHN *and* ISABELLA, *another* GUARD *now with them. The carriage is substantial/magic enough that a range of* MERRY MEN *can continually pop out from within it.*

WASSAIL, WASSAIL THROUGH THE FOREST DEEP
WHILE IN THE TOWN THE CHILDREN SLEEP
BUT WE HAVE PROMISES TO KEEP
WASSAIL! WASSAIL!

OPEN UP, OPEN UP
LET US FEAST, LET US SUP
IN THE DEEP, IN THE DARK
OPEN YOUR HEART!

OPEN UP, OPEN UP
FILL THIS BOWL, FILL THIS CUP,
IN THE DEPTH OF THE NIGHT
SEND US HOME WITH LIGHT!

WASSAIL, WASSAIL, THOUGH THERE'S NO ONE HERE
THE WOODS ARE WHITE AND THE SKIES ARE CLEAR
SING OUT, SING OUT, SING OUT YOUR FEAR
WASSAIL! WASSAIL!

RING OUT THE BELL
RING OUT LIKE HELL
CLEAR IN THE NIGHT
FAR OUT OF SIGHT

ICE ON THE GROUND
THUNDEROUS SOUND
ON, ON WE GO
POUNDING THE SNOW

NO STOPPING NOW
NO MATTER HOW
FASTER WE FLY
STARS IN THE SKY

NO LOOKING BACK
ICY AND BLACK

WIND STARTS TO WAIL
TOO FAR TO FAIL

OPEN UP, OPEN UP
LET US FEAST, LET US SUP
IN THE DEEP, IN THE DARK
OPEN YOUR HEART!

OPEN UP, OPEN UP
FILL THIS BOWL, FILL THIS CUP,
WHEN THE MOON GROWS PALE
HEAR OUR SWEET WASSAIL!

Song ends.

Scene Four

Still in the carriage, now a little outside the castle. Still travelling at speed.

ISABELLA. Where are you taking us?

PRINCE JOHN. We have to turn back. We have to get my gold!

DRIVER. Oh, don't worry about that, Your Highness.

The DRIVER *pulls their hood down. It is, of course,* ROBIN.

ROBIN. Nice work, team.

The 'GUARDS' remove their helmets too. It's SCARLETT *and* LITTLE JOHN.

SCARLETT. Cheers.

LITTLE JOHN. Got a bit dicey back there.

ROBIN. Always under control.

SCARLETT (*to* PRINCE JOHN). Hiya. You alright?

PRINCE JOHN. Wait – hold on – I don't think you're real guards.

SCARLETT. Yeah, busted – sorry. I'm Scarlett. I would curtsy but it's quite a small carriage and I don't have the full range of movement.

LITTLE JOHN (*to* ISABELLA). How're you doing?

ISABELLA. I've had better days.

LITTLE JOHN. Yeah, that's fair.

PRINCE JOHN. Are we being abducted?

ROBIN. Oh, he's a sharp one.

PRINCE JOHN. I demand –

ROBIN. Just hold tight, Your Majesty – this won't take long.

ISABELLA. But who are you?

ROBIN (*turning back to face them*). They call me the Robin.

ROBIN is expecting some recognition from this. It doesn't come.

SCARLETT. They're not local. They don't know who that is.

ROBIN. Oh, right. Oh, Marian's right – that is a bit annoying. (*To the* PRINCE.) You know I'm on posters and everything.

PRINCE JOHN. Are you?

Popping up somewhere behind them come PARSNIP *and* PARTRIDGE.

PARSNIP. Bit cramped in here, isn't it?

PRINCE JOHN *and* ISABELLA *both jump*.

PARTRIDGE. Sorry – didn't mean to startle you.

PARSNIP. Where's Marian? Did her team get out?

ROBIN. They shouldn't be far behind us.

PARTRIDGE. Hey – did you see me with that flaming arrow? Straight into the pudding – pow! Went up like a bonfire.

SCARLETT. That'll teach them to use that much brandy.

ROBIN. You all did very well. (*Over his shoulder.*) How's everyone getting on back there?

PARSNIP. Yeah, all good.

PRINCE JOHN. Sorry – not to bang on about it, but have we been kidnapped?

ROBIN. No! You've just been... borrowed, that's all – you won't come to any harm while you're with us – you have my word.

PARSNIP (*to* ISABELLA). Are you a princess?

LITTLE JOHN. Technically she's a countess.

PARSNIP. Oh. Is that not as good?

PARTRIDGE (*to* ISABELLA). Can I have one of your rings?

ROBIN. Don't be rude.

PARTRIDGE. What? She's got lots of them.

SCARLETT. That is true – you probably wouldn't miss one, would you?

PRINCE JOHN. Are we being robbed?

LITTLE JOHN. No! (*Beat.*) Oh, actually I'm not sure. Are they?

ROBIN. Can you be robbed of anything that wasn't truly yours to begin with?

ISABELLA. So that's a yes?

LITTLE JOHN. Maybe. Events are still unfolding.

ISABELLA. Right. Fantastic.

ROBIN. But try not to let that spoil your visit.

PARSNIP. How are you enjoying your time in Sherwood so far?

PRINCE JOHN. Oh, it's lovely.

PARSNIP. Isn't it?

SCARLETT. Now don't feel like you have to say that.

PRINCE JOHN. Always a blessing to get away from court. People live in such a bubble there.

ISABELLA. The castle was very draughty.

ROBIN. Oh, I'm sorry to hear that.

ISABELLA. And it had a very peculiar smell.

PARTRIDGE. Yeah, my mum thinks it's the moat.

PRINCE JOHN. Yes – didn't I say that? I said the moat looked funny.

ISABELLA. No one knows how to maintain a moat these days, that's the problem. Everyone likes the idea of having one – 'oh, just think how nice it'll be in the summer' – sure, in Provence, but with the weather here... Well – you know how it is.

SCARLETT. We're not really moat people.

ISABELLA. Right, yes, of course.

PRINCE JOHN. So to be clear – you're *not* robbing us?

ROBIN. Sorry, sorry, easily distracted – funny old day. Right gang, what do we think? Are we robbing the Prince? All equal under the hood, so a show of hands –

All raise their hands.

SCARLETT. Don't let go of the reins!

ROBIN. Sorry! Was that unanimous?

LITTLE JOHN. I think so.

ROBIN. Right, okay, so yes – bit of bad news for you, maybe – it is increasingly looking like you're being robbed. But you could just think of it as making your own contribution to the smooth running of the kingdom.

PRINCE JOHN. Who are you people?

ROBIN. I'm glad you asked. I would like to take a moment to talk to you about where your donations will be going.

PRINCE JOHN. Oh just take it. Forget I asked.

ROBIN. Now just how familiar are you with the basic tenets of anarcho-socialism?

PRINCE JOHN *sighs*.

LITTLE JOHN. Robin?

ROBIN. Yes?

LITTLE JOHN. On your left!

ROBIN. Yes, these ideas do emerge from a leftist school of thought, but in essence –

LITTLE JOHN. No, look!

An arrow thuds into the left side of the carriage.

SCARLETT. Duck and cover!

A couple more arrows hit the carriage.

ROBIN. One moment. (*To* SCARLETT.) Can you take over?

SCARLETT. Right, sure. Well feudalism is just one popular form of governance based upon –

ROBIN. No, take the reins!

SCARLETT. Oh, right. On it.

SCARLETT *takes the reins and* ROBIN *stands to shoot some arrows off. Before he can, a war cry, and four more stags/scooters zoom on, ridden by* MARIAN, MUCH, PEAR *and* PLUM *with* BERRY, SPROUT, NUTMEG *and* CLOVE *clinging to their backs. They have their own bows drawn.*

MARIAN. Don't worry, Robin, we'll pick them off!

ROBIN. Oh! You took your time!

PEAR. We just had to stash away the treasure first.

LITTLE JOHN. You got it all out then?

MUCH. No sweat.

CLOVE. I hit a man with a swan.

SCARLETT. Good for you.

PRINCE JOHN. Oh God, is that the child actors again?

BERRY. Is that the Princess?

PARSNIP. Nah, she's only a countess.

BERRY (*disappointed*). Oh.

MARIAN. We'll see you back at the base. Come on, gang!

More hooting and hollering, as they charge off again.

ISABELLA. So this is what you do, is it? You just ride around taking other people's things?

PARTRIDGE. No, that's what the Sheriff does.

PRINCE JOHN. Do you have my gold? Did you take my gold?!

SCARLETT. What makes it yours?

PRINCE JOHN. That money had been earmarked to ensure the future stability of the nation!

ROBIN. Ah yes, good old trickle-down economics. We favour a grassroots approach.

ISABELLA. Just let me keep this ring please – my grandmother gave it to me.

SCARLETT. What did the Sheriff let us keep?

PARSNIP. She's not the Sheriff though.

SCARLETT. She might be even worse. You don't know.

PARTRIDGE. Neither do you.

ISABELLA. We're actually both very nice people, actually.

SCARLETT. You would say that.

PRINCE JOHN. We are! You know I didn't ask to be Prince. I didn't choose any of this. I don't want to be traipsing up and down the country trying to keep everybody happy

because my stupid big brother is off fighting his silly Holy
War! I think it's very unfair, actually, for you to judge me –
or her – based on the circumstances *we were born into*,
yeah? And actually it's really horrible of you to say 'oh well
you're probably a bad person' just because of who are
parents are, or the roles that society assigned to us, when
actually we didn't get a say in it, and none of that should
really make any difference to anything!

Beat.

PARSNIP. Wow. Did we just make the Prince an anarcho-socialist?

PARTRIDGE. I don't know. Maybe. (*To* PRINCE JOHN.) Keep going.

PRINCE JOHN. And I'm sorry, but whoever you are and whatever you might want, there's a proper way to go about things, and just jumping into someone's carriage uninvited and starting to take their things is actually incredibly rude!

ROBIN. I understand.

PRINCE JOHN. You do?

ROBIN. Oh I do. I'm afraid the ruling classes have always valued civility above justice.

SCARLETT. Amen.

ISABELLA. No, he's right. I think if you actually *talked* to people reasonably – explained… I had a maid. It turned out she couldn't afford to feed her family. She told me, and I made sure they got fed. She didn't *steal*.

SCARLETT. And what if you hadn't helped her?

ROBIN. Great question.

ISABELLA. But I did.

SCARLETT. But if you hadn't? Or if she had a different mistress who'd looked on her less kindly? Would you have expected her to starve politely?

LITTLE JOHN. I think we've lost them.

ROBIN. No – they can grasp this.

LITTLE JOHN. No, the guards who were chasing – I think we've lost them all. Marian's team drew them off us.

ROBIN. Oh, good. I'll just take us a little further in.

PRINCE JOHN. What are you going to do with us?

ROBIN. Nothing. We got what we needed from you. Scarlett will go with you until you're in sight of the castle.

PARTRIDGE. What if they come back? What if they hurt more people, trying to find us?

ISABELLA. We won't.

PARTRIDGE. We don't know them.

ROBIN. And they don't know us. But let's imagine for a moment that we're all better than we might sometimes fear. I hope you know this was nothing personal, Your Majesties – in fact it's very simple. There are a lot of folk round here with nothing, and one or two with a great deal, and as you so rightly observe, the family you're born into shouldn't dictate the life you lead. (*To* ISABELLA.) That's a very pretty ring. You take good care of it.

ISABELLA. I will.

ROBIN. This should do.

He pulls on the reins. A sense of the carriage stopping.

(*To* LITTLE JOHN.) Sound the horn – let them know we're here.

LITTLE JOHN *blows a horn.*

PRINCE JOHN. Well, this has been... deeply unpleasant. Can we go now?

ROBIN. You can. (*To* SCARLETT.) Help them down.

They all get out of the carriage.

SCARLETT (*to* PRINCE JOHN). I'm going to have to blindfold you for the way back.

PRINCE JOHN. Of course. Wonderful.

MUCH *and* MARIAN *enter with the younger* CHILDREN, *and* PEAR *and* PLUM. *They're pulling a sled loaded up with bulging hessian sacks.*

MARIAN. Come on! Not much further. (*To the others.*) All in one piece?

ROBIN. Just about.

PRINCE JOHN (*spotting the sled*). Is that my gold?!

PLUM (*deadpan*). Why would you think that.

ISABELLA. Come on, let's just leave.

SPROUT. Wait!

PRINCE JOHN. What now?

SPROUT *produces a glittery pinecone hedgehog, or some such. They hand it to the* PRINCE.

SPROUT. Here.

PRINCE JOHN. What's this?

SPROUT. For you. For Christmas. The Sheriff squished it, but I fixed it again.

PRINCE JOHN. What do I do with it?

SPROUT. It's a gift.

PRINCE JOHN. Oh.

ISABELLA. Thank you. I'll treasure it.

SPROUT. Merry Christmas.

ISABELLA. Merry Christmas.

ROBIN. Safe travels, Your Majesty.

PRINCE JOHN. I want to be clear that I haven't enjoyed this at all. Merry Christmas.

SCARLETT. This way.

SCARLETT *leads* ISABELLA *and* PRINCE JOHN *off.*

ROBIN. So – did you get everything out?

MARIAN. Everything on my list.

LITTLE JOHN. Everything?

PLUM. You won't believe it.

PEAR. Never seen so much.

ROBIN. But remember, it's not all for us.

ROBIN *opens up one sack. We see it's full of the colourful stockings, now all bulging.*

There's one of these for every family in town. We need to make sure everyone gets their share. (*To* MARIAN.) You coming?

MARIAN. Absolutely. Just let me grab –

She's cut off.

PLUM. Marian – can you help with the fire?

SPROUT. Marian, Marian, I need to make another hedgehog.

LITTLE JOHN. Where are we going to stash all this?

PARTRIDGE. Marian, did you see me shoot that pudding?

PARSNIP. Marian, I don't want to make a fuss, but I think I did get hit by about seven arrows. Just grazes mostly.

MARIAN. Right, right. (*Beat.*) Actually, Robin can deal with all that.

PARSNIP. Really?

ROBIN. Really?

MARIAN. Of course he can. (*To* ROBIN.) You've got this. I'll get all these dropped off. Back soon.

MARIAN *goes, the carriage somehow vanishing with her.*

Scene Five

The Great Oak. As the COMPANY *sing, the tree is decorated with ribbons, garlands, candles/paper lanterns and all other sorts of handmade decorations – the very first Christmas tree. Properly magical, full of wonder. Maybe more stockings are laid out/hung off the branches too. Midway through the song,* MARIAN *returns. Embraces, celebrations, etc.*

MERRY.
DECK THE BOUGHS WITH HOLLY BERRY
FA-LA-LA-LA-LA LA-LA-LA-LA
'TIS THE SEASON TO BE MERRY
FA-LA-LA-LA-LA LA-LA-LA-LA

HERE THE OAK AND HERE THE HAZEL
FA-LA-LA, LA-LA-LA, LA-LA-LAH
DECORATE OUR CHRISTMAS TABLE
FA-LA-LA-LA-LA LA-LA-LA-LA

MARIAN. How are you getting on here?

MUCH. We could do with more water.

SPROUT. I'll go. Don't start without me.

SPROUT *runs off.*

MERRY.
TOAST THE LORDS AND TOAST THE PRINCES
FA-LA-LA-LA-LA LA-LA-LA-LA
TOAST THE SHERIFF'S PENNY PINCHES
FA-LA-LA-LA-LA LA-LA-LA-LA

THOUGH THEY TRIED THEIR BEST TO THWART US
FA-LA-LA, LA-LA-LA, LA-LA-LA
THEY CAN'T STOP THE YULETIDE CHORUS
FA-LA-LA-LA-LA LA-LA-LA-LA
FA-LA-LA-LA-LA, LA-LA –

Song is interrupted by the arrival of the SHERIFF *and* GUARDS. *The* SHERIFF *clutches* SPROUT *and holds a knife to their throat. The* SHERIFF *is covered in mud and scratches. He's gone wild.*

SHERIFF. There you all are.

SCARLETT. Drop it.

SHERIFF. Nobody move.

ROBIN (*to* SPROUT). Are you hurt? Has he hurt you?

SPROUT. No.

SHERIFF. Put your weapons down. Any bows, knives, sticks, staffs, anything. Don't try anything clever.

ROBIN. Whatever you say.

ROBIN *does as ordered*.

SHERIFF. Good.

ROBIN. If you hurt so much as a hair –

SHERIFF (*suddenly very loud*). I AM TALKING NOW, ROBIN HOOD!

ROBIN. Yes, Sheriff.

SHERIFF. You thought you could outrun me, but I'll always track you down. You thought you could hide out here, but these are *my* woods – mine!

LITTLE JOHN. These woods are everybody's.

SHERIFF. Listen to me! You think this is all great fun, do you? All a game? Having your adventures, your great larks? That ends tonight. You will do as you're told, or you will die. Understood?

PARSNIP. So I'll die.

SHERIFF (*calmly*). Sage, start making a list of the ones who're choosing death.

ROBIN. I… I am Robin of the Hood. Outlaw. Outsider. I act alone. I always have.

MARIAN. Robin –

ROBIN. So take me in, leave everyone else in peace –

ACT TWO, SCENE FIVE   87

SHERIFF. No, it's far too late for that. These children had bright futures once, but *you* stole that from them. The older ones will be readied for war – King Richard needs more soldiers in the Holy Land. The younger will be put to work here. Each lord or lady will take a different child away with them, to ensure there can be no further collusion – clearly it's too dangerous to keep any of you together.

PEAR. You can't do that.

PLUM. She's my sister.

SHERIFF. Then say your farewells.

SCARLETT. We won't go.

SHERIFF. You will, and you shall prove more useful to your new masters intact, but don't test me. You can still work without a tongue, after all.

SCARLETT. You know those toffs back at the castle are never going to like you?

SHERIFF. Quiet!

SCARLETT. It'll never be enough for them.

SHERIFF. I said silence!

SCARLETT. Why do you want to impress them? Why are you on their side?

SHERIFF (*to* ROBIN/MARIAN). This – you see this is your doing. You've never taught them respect, or obedience. You've poisoned their minds, encouraged their rebellion, taught them they could have anything they wanted without ever having to work for it – just take, take, take, lie, cheat, steal – anarchy! What do you even want with the Prince's gold anyway? You can't spend it – we'd find you the moment you tried to. You think you're so clever, so pure, so *good*, but you're as greedy as anyone. Greedy and stupid. Let's see what we have here.

The SHERIFF *empties out a big sack that came in with Marian on the sled. Instead of gold/treasure, etc., it's full of fresh fruit and vegetables, a bit of meat, cheeses, pies, all edible produce.*

Where is it? The gold – what have you done with it?

ROBIN. It's not here.

SHERIFF. Don't lie to me!

The SHERIFF *empties out some of the stockings – again, it's all just produce.*

(*To the* GUARDS.) Search everywhere! Set the whole forest on fire if you have to. (*Back to* ROBIN.) Tell me, before I make you regret it.

MUCH. The gold never came here.

SHERIFF. Take out her eye.

LITTLE JOHN. It's true!

ROBIN. The gold is still in the castle! In the keep, where you left it.

SHERIFF. You expect me to believe that?

ROBIN. You posted an entire garrison outside. The walls are solid stone. There was never any way to it – you made sure of that.

SHERIFF. I don't believe you. You've hidden it somewhere.

ROBIN. We never went for the gold. Any kind of commotion and you'd go into lockdown – you'd double the guard – but you know where no one's looking?

SHERIFF. Where?

MARIAN. The kitchens. We could walk straight in and help ourselves to anything we needed.

ROBIN. I rode out in the Prince's carriage – a whole garrison chased after us.

MARIAN. And no one noticed us slipping out the back with enough fresh food to feed an army. Packed it away in the snow until the coast was clear.

SHERIFF. But why?

SCARLETT. Why do you think?

SHERIFF. You really expect me to believe you all risked your lives for what? For *this*? For royal leftovers? For scraps?

PARSNIP. There was plenty more before we shared it out.

LITTLE JOHN. We had to make sure every family in the parish got something.

SHERIFF. No. This is absurd.

MARIAN. It's true, I swear it.

SHERIFF. You did all this for a meal?

ROBIN. You said it yourself – what are we going to do with gold? They're just hungry. (*Beat.*) Leave the food for them. Please. Take me away – take my life if you have to, but just let them eat. I promised them.

SHERIFF. No, this is... is... This is still a trick – a ruse.

ROBIN. I saw your larders – it won't be missed.

SAGE. Sir?

SHERIFF. What is it?

SAGE. No gold anywhere.

EGG. No other food either.

SHERIFF. That doesn't prove anything. Where do you actually live? We'll have to search their houses.

NOG. They don't have houses, sir.

SHERIFF. Come on! Everyone has a house!

EGG. No, sir. Not here.

SHERIFF. Well they can't live out here – not in the winter – in the middle of winter. Where's the stove, where's the bedding? You said no food anywhere?

ONION. A few acorns. Something dried and green.

MARIAN. Nettle leaves.

ONION. Right.

MARIAN. We make a broth from them.

SHERIFF. No, but… (*Remembering something*.) Aha! You said some of their parents work in the castle – they'll sleep in the castle then, in the warm – right under our noses.

SAGE. Only servants can sleep in the castle, sir – no children allowed.

SHERIFF. But… but…

MUCH. It's not so bad in the summer. And we try to preserve what we can.

LITTLE JOHN. But there are more of us now. This winter caught us off guard.

CLOVE. We could share it with you, if you wanted.

SHERIFF. What?

NUTMEG. There might even be *leftovers*.

SHERIFF (*angry, as a way to hold back tears – to* MARIAN). You said you were looking after them! When I came here before –

MARIAN. We are, as best we can.

SHERIFF. All this for a piece of bread? A link of sausage?

BERRY. There's *sausage*?

SHERIFF. For sprouts?

CLOVE. Sprouts are the best bit.

SPROUT. Thanks.

ROBIN. I promised them a feast. I promised that we'd eat like kings.

The SHERIFF *breaks down, fully crying*.

EGG. Sir?

ACT TWO, SCENE FIVE   91

SHERIFF. Go.

NOG. What?

SHERIFF. All of you – go. Now.

ONION. What about them?

SHERIFF. There is no gold here. No evidence of any crime committed. It's late, and it's Christmas. Go home.

All the GUARDS *go. The* SHERIFF *is still very shaken. He tries his best to collect himself.*

You see this mark on my hand? I was eight or nine, maybe. I'd been living on the streets for years already. I can't remember when I'd last eaten. But it was Christmas Day – I didn't know it was Christmas until I smelt the goose cooking. Watched it turn for hours on a spit, transfixed. Watched as this fine family tucked in, made merry, toasted their good fortune, then threw the carcass out for their dogs. But there was still so much meat on it, you see, and I was so hungry. I could make it last for days – not just for me, I had friends I was eager to share my bounty with – I had friends back then. A nightwatchman caught me with it, gripped tight against my chest, still warm, hot grease smeared down me. This is the mark of a thief. I was lucky they didn't take a finger. So I vowed – I promised myself I would never disgrace myself like that again. Orphan or not, I would become upstanding, respectable, feared – a man of law. I would show the world I was worth something. Because the shame I felt that day – I've never known anything like it. At least not until right now.

ROBIN. Are you staying for dinner, Sheriff?

SHERIFF. What?

ROBIN. Always space for one more.

SCARLETT. He doesn't deserve it.

SHERIFF. She's right, I don't.

ROBIN. If we only save our kindness for the ones who deserve it, it isn't worth anything at all. (*Back to the* SHERIFF.) Sit for a while, at least. You're a long way from home.

SHERIFF. Yes.

MARIAN. Pear, Plum, you can start peeling the vegetables.

PARSNIP. And save all the trimmings for the gravy.

PLUM. We won't waste anything.

LITTLE JOHN. I'll get a fire going.

PARTRIDGE. We still need fresh water too.

NUTMEG. What can I do?

CLOVE. Do you need a taste-tester?

MARIAN. Certainly.

BERRY. Ooh, me too!

SHERIFF. How can I help you?

ROBIN. What are you like with a flint?

SHERIFF. I mean it. I need to help you. I have to.

SCARLETT (*still not letting the* SHERIFF *off the hook*). So you forgot what it was like to be hungry? What did you think was happening out here? You think we chose this?

SHERIFF. I'm sorry.

SCARLETT. I can't eat your apologies, can I?

MARIAN. Scarlett – it's Christmas.

SCARLETT. I'm not sharing a meal with him. Not him.

SHERIFF. Nor should you. I'll go. But I shan't forget this. I'll speak to the lords, to the Prince –

PARTRIDGE. To all those fancy folk who hate you?

SHERIFF. To anyone who'll listen. And if no one will, I'll take matters into my own hands. Enjoy your feast – you've earned it. Leave the rest to me.

SHERIFF *goes.* MUCH *leads the* COMPANY *in a song.*

ACT TWO, SCENE FIVE

Song: 'The Ballad of Saint Nicholas'

COMPANY.
ONCE IN THE TOWN OF NOTTINGHAM
A LONG, LONG TIME AGO
THERE LIVED A MAN NAMED NICHOLAS
BUT NOT THE ONE YOU KNOW

DEEP IN HIS HEART A SHARD OF ICE
A SOMBRE MAN OF LAW
BUT THEN UPON A WINTER NIGHT
THAT ICE BEGAN TO THAW

Back in the castle. The SHERIFF *calls out.*

SHERIFF. Gorse! Bramble!

GORSE *and* BRAMBLE *enter.*

BRAMBLE. Here, sire.

GORSE. Did you catch the Robin?

SHERIFF. Not tonight. Maybe next time.

BRAMBLE. I hear he's not a man at all, some faerie, some pixie, some creature of the forest.

SHERIFF. Perhaps.

GORSE. And he has an army of elves to help him – magic elves who do whatever he bids them.

SHERIFF. Magical elves? Yes, well then I suppose we never stood a chance. Any more disturbances?

BRAMBLE. No sir. The Prince and the Countess got back a little while ago.

GORSE. And no one's come near the keep. A full garrison still positioned outside.

SHERIFF. Good. Good. I'll make my own checks. Bring me my riding cloak.

Another verse of song. During this, the SHERIFF *is brought a long, hooded cloak in a deep forest green with a gold trim. Very festive.*

COMPANY.
> OLD NICK WAS QUITE THE DEVIL ONCE
> WHO RULED WITH IRON FIST
> AND WOE BETIDE THE FOE WHO FALLS
> UPON HIS NAUGHTY LIST
>
> BUT IN THE FOREST DARK AND DEEP
> A ROBIN SHONE A LIGHT
> NOW HE HAS PROMISES TO KEEP
> AND MANY WRONGS TO RIGHT
> IF YOU'RE GOOD, IF YOU'RE GOOD...

Outside the castle keep. SAGE *and* ONION *stand guard. The* SHERIFF *approaches.*

SHERIFF. Wake up – you're not off duty yet.

SAGE. Sir! Good evening, sir!

SHERIFF. The castle has already been infiltrated once tonight – we can't trust what the Robin said – we need to take our own precautions. Follow me.

ONION. Yes, sir.

COMPANY.
> IF YOU'RE GOOD, IF YOU'RE GOOD
> WHO'S THAT THERE BENEATH THE HOOD?
> IN THE COLD, IN THE DARK
> JUST ENOUGH TO LIGHT A SPARK

SHERIFF, SAGE *and* ONION *now at the stables with* NOG. *They struggle under the weight of gold.*

NOG. And you're sure about this?

SHERIFF. We can't use any of the horses for this – can't draw any attention.

NOG. To what? (*Beat – clocking the bags.*) Is that the gold for the Prince?

SHERIFF. None of your business. Breathe a word of this to anyone –

NOG. No sir – of course not, sir.

SHERIFF (*now softly*). It's going back to where it belongs.
I know I haven't given you any reason to trust me, but trust me – please.

EGG *enters, leading* RUDOLPH *on*.

EGG. Easy, easy. (*To* SHERIFF.) You think you can ride him?

SHERIFF. Time to find out, I suppose.

The SHERIFF *approaches* RUDOLPH. *He shrinks back*.

Steady on now. You want a carrot?

EGG. He prefers mince pies.

SHERIFF. Then you're in luck.

He fishes a mince pie out of a pocket.

There now. Dark night tonight. We've got a long ride ahead, and you know these woods better than I do, so you're going to have to guide me, alright?

RUDOLPH *and the* SHERIFF *seem to come to some kind of agreement*.

Good chap. Thank you, friends. Merry Christmas.

The SHERIFF *and* RUDOLPH *ride off*.

COMPANY.
OLD NICK KNOWS WHAT MAKES PEOPLE TICK
THOUGH YOU MIGHT FIND IT STRANGE
HE KNOWS IF YOU'VE BEEN BAD OR GOOD
HE KNOWS THAT YOU CAN CHANGE

HE KNOWS THAT WE ALL MAKE MISTAKES
BUT STILL CAN MAKE AMENDS
HE KNOWS THE GREATEST WEALTH THERE IS
IS WEALTH THAT'S SHARED WITH FRIENDS

The SHERIFF *cracks a whip*.

SHERIFF. Hah!

SHERIFF/COMPANY.
  IF YOU'RE GOOD, IF YOU'RE GOOD
  WHO'S THAT THERE BENEATH THE HOOD?
  IN THE COLD, IN THE DARK
  JUST ENOUGH TO LIGHT A SPARK
  IF YOU'RE GOOD, IF YOU'RE GOOD
  THERE IS HOPE
  WHO'S THAT THERE BENEATH THE HOOD?
  HERE HE COMES
  IN THE COLD, IN THE DARK
  THERE IS HOPE
  JUST ENOUGH TO LIGHT A SPARK

Back in the heart of the forest. The SHERIFF *with* ROBIN, MARIAN, *etc.* RUDOLPH *is loaded up with gold.*

ROBIN. You just rode out with all of it?

SHERIFF. Every last penny.

SCARLETT. And how are you giving it out now?

SHERIFF. I've got my ways. I've been through the town already, placing a few coins into the shoes of little children while they sleep. Over rooftops, down chimneys, a little here and there wherever I can.

MARIAN. That's remarkable.

SHERIFF. Next year – next year I'll be more prepared.

PARSNIP. You're going to do this next year as well?

SHERIFF. And the year after. For as many Christmases as I have. I'll have to be clever.

PARTRIDGE. Puddings!

PARSNIP. Why are you always thinking about puddings?

PARTRIDGE. No, but you could hide some gold in them – get a baker to put a coin in every pudding or every loaf they make – no one would ever think to look there.

PEAR. My mum could help with that.

ACT TWO, SCENE FIVE

LITTLE JOHN (*to the* SHERIFF). But what'll you do now? You know you can't go back to the castle – can't go back to being the Sheriff. It won't be long before –

A sharp cut to the palace, where PRINCE JOHN *and* ISABELLA *have just discovered the gold is missing.*

PRINCE JOHN. My gold! It's gone – they did take it!

ISABELLA. Maybe they were right – maybe it was never yours to begin with.

PRINCE JOHN. No, that's it – I've had it – I'm going to invade France.

PRINCE JOHN *storms off,* ISABELLA *follows – we cut back to the forest.*

MUCH. I'm sure they'll get over it.

LITTLE JOHN (*to the* SHERIFF). You can stay here with us, if you like.

SHERIFF. That's very kind.

NUTMEG. At least until you've built me a new birdhouse.

SHERIFF. I'll bring you one next Christmas. I'll visit again then. Nottingham isn't the only town with needy children – especially in winter, when we need the light the most.

SCARLETT. Sheriff?

SHERIFF. I don't think I'm a sheriff any more.

SCARLETT. So what do we call you?

SHERIFF. Just Nicholas is fine.

SCARLETT. Alright, Nicholas. So you're not staying in the forest?

SHERIFF. No.

SCARLETT. You won't be needing that cloak then.

MARIAN. Scarlett –

SHERIFF. No, you're right.

He takes off the green cloak.

Here – keep yourself warm.

SCARLETT. Wait there.

SCARLETT *goes to some secret hiding spot behind the oak and pulls out a deep-red cloak with white fur trim – the archetypal Father Christmas look. She hands it to the* SHERIFF.

It was my dad's. Can't really use it out here because it does make you stand out a bit, but it's about time somebody else wore it.

SHERIFF. I couldn't.

SCARLETT. It's a good colour for a robin. You might not be our Robin, but you still count.

SHERIFF. Thank you. I'll treasure it.

SCARLETT. That's alright. Merry Christmas.

ROBIN. Merry Christmas, Nicholas.

SHERIFF. Merry Christmas, Robin. Merry Christmas, one and all.

COMPANY.
AND THOUGH IT ALL BEGAN THAT NIGHT
SAINT NICHOLAS OF FAME
HAD MANY YEARS OF TOIL AHEAD
BEFORE HE EARNED THAT NAME

A SCARLET CLOAK TO KEEP HIM WARM
AS RED AS ROBIN'S BREAST
AND WHISKERS WHITE AS DRIVEN SNOW
YOU SURELY KNOW THE REST

IF YOU'RE GOOD, IF YOU'RE GOOD
WHO'S THAT THERE BENEATH THE HOOD?
IN THE COLD, IN THE DARK
JUST ENOUGH TO LIGHT A SPARK

IF YOU'RE GOOD, IF YOU'RE GOOD
THERE IS HOPE
WHO'S THAT THERE BENEATH THE HOOD?
HERE HE COMES
IN THE COLD, IN THE DARK
THERE IS HOPE
JUST ENOUGH TO LIGHT A SPARK

KEEP ON TRUDGING THE SNOW DOWN
KEEP ON STANDING STRONG
KEEP SOME FIRE IN YOUR BELLY
AND IN YOUR HEART A SONG
IN THE WINTER LONG AGO

Ends.

www.nickhernbooks.co.uk

@nickhernbooks